# THE
# BIRD
# BOOK
## ALMA'S STORY

PATSY LEVANG

Printed in the United States of America.

Library of Congress Control Number:  2010913999

ISBN          Paperback          978-1-965881-05-7
              Hardback           978-1-965881-06-4
              eBook              978-1-965881-07-1


**Boundless Script Inc**
99 Wall Street #210
New York, NY, 10005

www.boundlessscript.com

# Contents

# *Prologue*

To tell her story, she only had the bird book. She left it unfinished, just like her life appeared to be. The question of who she was prompted me to begin searching for answers. Had I known about the scrapbook of Alma's I would have started years ago to tell her story. I refused to have her life and legacy forgotten, and with this in mind, I wrote the Bird Book, Alma's Story. Some may argue that I shouldn't encroach on the domain of a deceased individual, however, it has always been in me to find out the answers, and so for that reason, Alma's story must be told. She left her story in the phrases she had composed. In the pieces of artwork she created, she left her story behind. She left her story in the memories of those who knew her, of whom there are very few.

# *Opening*

She was shy, beyond most normal definitions of the word. Many of the interactions people had with her reflected this. Linda and Harold arrived at the farmhouse in Minnesota to spend some time with the family. "Hey, how ya doin'?" asked Harold. He enfolded Lena in his big hug and almost simultaneously reached out a very large hand to shake Harry's extended hand. Alma had peeked around the corner of her bedroom door at the sound of all the commotion, then disappeared. Alma did not speak to him, and she barely let her eyes flicker in his direction.

"Well, how are you?" Harold queried a little more quietly, with a big, friendly smile. Harold moved back, the smile fading from his face; he knew he was not to intrude. Not a word had been said.

Harold and Linda had been to the farm before. Each time they tried to visit with her, Alma said nothing, except for a small sound she made in place of a greeting. Linda had only been to the farm a few times, and conversation was all one-way with Alma. Despite Linda's best efforts, she was unable to recall the few words that Alma had spoken. When interviewing other relatives, it became clear that the experience Linda and Harold had was similar to all the others; Alma did not speak, only when she wanted to, and that seemed to be never.

The bird book was in my thoughts. From the moment that it came into my possession, I knew it held the story of the anonymous little family. When I first got it, Alma had passed away. She was in bed at the end and did not speak. When the book arrived in my home, I put it on a shelf, and then I began thinking about how I could finish the book. Alma's family wanted me to have it. My cousins wanted me to finish the artwork that had never quite reached completion. Perhaps Alma desperately wished for someone to tell the story within its pages. The story is hers, and this influenced my approach. It was probably the hope she had of bringing her love for birds to others. Many times, I got the book down and began planning how I would finish the artwork in it. I thought about what mediums I would use. I never gave much thought to the task of completing the written story that lay beneath the silent pictures of the birds and her sparse prose. Alma had used watercolor, pencil, and colored pencil. Many of the pictures were unfinished. While many of the pictures displayed a mature style, others had a childlike quality. They might very well have been copies of something she saw somewhere; I will never know. She had started the book in 1960. She appeared to want to tell someone how her life had gone and how much she had to share with the world. She quit working on the book in 1980.

The work began a full fifty years ago. Alma is dead, as are Henry, Lena, Dena, Esther, Julia, and Harry. In 1919, a tornado struck Julia, the fifth child, on the head with a piece of wood, leading to her institutionalization. No one really knew what else to do. Julia went into silence at that point, sealing her part of the family's untold story forever. Julia's silence ended long before Alma's death. All seven of Helmer's children have died. They left no children behind. Four of the seven children never married at all. Alma was one of the four who never married. In Alma's pristine world of birds and silence, there could be no unwanted intrusions except by means of the books she read; many of them must have been about birds, but they were not among the things that were sent to me. I hold the one key to understanding anything about her life beyond the walls and the door.

In July 1994, I traveled to Minnesota to visit two of Alma's cousins. I was hoping to find out more about her so that I could finish the bird book and publish it. Louise and Edna said that Alma was extremely shy. They told me a little bit about her. This is what they told me. "Before Alma became ill, the pastor came to give her communion. It took many visits before she came out of her room and went to the kitchen table, where she eventually took communion. Generally, her room was the destination for her food. She would stay in her room and peek around the corner when company came. If anyone looked directly at her, she would turn away. She would never look at you when you tried to speak to her." There wasn't much that Edna and Louise could tell me. Alma's sisters and brothers had protected and cared for her all of her life. If any one of them knew why Alma was the way she was, they never said. They were a kind, caring family. Her only hope to communicate with the world lay buried in the pages of the bird book. She had lived in a prison she made for herself, and rarely did a shaft of light penetrate that prison. There was a time when there were no prison walls, according to notes written by the family. As a young girl, Alma appeared to be a happy, carefree youngster, just like so many young people are. Somewhere, along the path to adulthood, something drastically changed for Alma. Can we conclude that Alma experienced some form of mental aberration? No, I do not believe that there is evidence to support such a conclusion. Gradually, she started spending more and more of her time in her bedroom, and one day she just stopped coming out altogether. What was it that made her quit living as we imagined? What made her so completely reclusive that dealing with people became a task she simply refused to attempt? Alma went to sleep during the summer of 1986. She died that summer, in the safety of her room. The birds she loved so much lived close by her window. One can imagine that she closed her eyes in eternal rest to the multiplicity of birds singing outside her room.

The Bird Book tells the stories of her real friends. She left no descendants, with the exception of her birds. She only knew a few simple words to accompany the bird book. Those words give her actual insight into her heart and soul. The rest of the few facts there seem to have come from others' impressions of her. Her intricate, finely woven lines of prose form a quiet fit with the bird book. The quilt top features official state flowers embroidered on unbleached muslin in each block. We've preserved it as a tribute to Alma. The story revolves around a woman who receives minimal attention. I noticed her, and I want you to notice her, too. I noticed her, and I want you to notice her, too. She loved birds, and she seemed to find freedom in these feathered friends. She either created the artwork surrounding the birds herself or copied it. If she copied the pictures, I have no idea to whom the credit should go. Her siblings lived with her, or at least near her. I don't believe their worlds intersected very much. The picturesque, lush lands of western Minnesota surrounded their farm. Ponds, trees, grasses, and plenty of wild flowers surrounded their home. Whatever seemed to keep Alma from interacting with the world also gave her the inspiration to live her life through the birds. I know many people who live their lives through nature or through other people. Alma deserves to have her story told. It is not life-changing, but it is also not forgettable in her life. Her life had value and meaning, and perhaps she will gain a bit of immortality because of the secrets her soul kept, which we can only glimpse through the bird pictures, which were all her own effort and design to the best of my knowledge. Alma's story is going to live through this book, and we will all be better for it.

A very tame bird, often seen close to the habitation of mankind where it feeds on the ground, digging out grubs from the roots of grass tufts. The Robin is migratory, arriving earliest in spring and leaving late in fall. It raises two broods of young a year. The Robin is dark grayish-brown above, and cinnamon-red below, white on neck. Common.

ROBIN

# Robin

She begins her journey with Robin. Robin, also known as the harbinger of spring, is a very appropriate first choice for her. Certainly, spring brings to mind the rebirth of life, and through the birds in her book, Alma was to find a life outside of her four walls. The Robin has also demonstrated a great fondness for humans and has enjoyed great popularity with humans everywhere they are cohabitants. Alma had a great deal of difficulty dealing with humans who entered her world; however, the fondness she felt for the society that often came close to her bedroom door was probably part of the reason she spent time peering around the corner of her door when company would arrive. When Alma drew the Robin and painted it with watercolors, she did not have a great deal of understanding of her medium. She probably wanted to bring as much life as she could to the picture, and she chose watercolors. The fact that the birds would come in the spring and leave again in the late fall on their farm in Minnesota must have been a great deal like the people that came to visit from time to time. It is very certain that Alma would spend time looking out her window, waiting for the arrival of the beloved Robin every spring. She also seemed very interested in people's arrivals, and much like Robin, when people get too close, Alma retreats inward, and communication with the outside world becomes virtually impossible. Her handwriting was meticulous, and she carefully selected the few words she wrote about Robin from her source.

## Her Words

"I love spring. I wish I could get out of my room and be with you, Robin friend. I can see you; at least, I think it is you. I can hear you; at least, I am sure it is your song. I see so many things that they do not think I notice."

CATBIRD

# Catbird

Alma loved cats, as evidenced by the fact that her tabby cat could wander unfettered into and out of her room. The next bird presents that part of her life. Her choice of the catbird once again calls to mind her interest in the people around her, because this bird dwells among men in much the same way as the robin. The catbird is very much like its feline compatriot. He demonstrates a catlike call, and during the nesting season, other birds are not very fond of this bird's voice. The Catbird's voice, which is not very much like a bird, is supported by the fact that he acts a lot like a cat. He slinks through the bushes and has a reputation as a nest robber. The catbird seems to have a great desire to "show off." I think deep in Alma's heart there was an unfulfilled wish to be like the catbird and have more dominion over the world around her. Like the catbird, she seemed to have a desire to be noticed and yet a debilitating self-consciousness that wouldn't allow such a display of behavior. The catbird's singing ability ranks third. He tends toward some loud, rather harsh sounds in his repertoire. Alma's rendering of the catbird makes him far more beautiful than he perhaps appears in nature. To Alma, his strength of personality gave him that extra measure of beauty and perhaps made him enviable because of her great fear of ever being that flamboyant.

## Her Words

"I think I sound a little like the catbird. The catbird is free; I love it. I wish I dared to look at people. They really scare me. He sits there, waiting and hoping that he will be able to rob the nest of some unsuspecting bird. I can just see him. I know what a careful mover he must be."

The woodthrush is a bird of the woodlands, a little smaller of size than the Robin. It has a clear 'flute-like' song.

There are five eastern species of Thrush's, and all are brown backed birds with spotted breasts, rather long legs for songbirds, large eyes, and moderately slender bills.

W·O·O·D·T·H·R·U·S·H

# Wood Thrush

It is so interesting that Alma would choose to present the wood thrush as the third bird in her book. Although the Wood Thrush prefers to live in a deeply wooded area, he often makes his home near human habitations. He presents himself as a great deal more shy and retiring than Robin; however, he seems to enjoy conducting his life activities near the homes of humans, in trees, or under shrubbery. The wood thrush is the only one of the thrushes that appears to be very interested in humans. It seems that this bird, like Alma, shared a desire to intermix with human society. I can believe that Alma saw something of herself in the lifestyle of this bird and that, through the characteristics of the bird, she was again reaching out to human society beyond her bedroom door. "The music of the Wood Thrush somewhat resembles the music written by a great composer," she said. Perhaps a great composer listened to the Wood Thrush's sweet refrain, drawing inspiration from it to compose music that encapsulated the sound. The Wood Thrush seems to enjoy foods that fit well with close proximity to humans. He eats fruit and insects and therefore does very well living in or near a garden where he can dine on insects and help the gardener. The wood thrush's eye is very distinctive, and it was probably another touch point for Alma. Her eye was distinctive, too. She was always aware of everything around her, frequently shifting her focus from the activity to the activity itself. Despite this, she maintained her attentiveness, quickly flicking her eyes in different directions to observe the happenings, all the while hoping no one would notice. Once again, it appears that Alma was desperately reaching out to her surroundings but could not find a way to really let the world know that she was interested.

## Her Words

"Today I worked on my plate of wood thrush. I love the wood thrush. It sees, and I see. I have plans for this book. One day, it will be amazing, overflowing with my bird friends and their stories. I know I only have to finish it. I get so tired."

# Bluebird

Her next bird companion is the bluebird. What a choice! This bird is yet another spring messenger. While many individuals of the Robin species do stay for the winter in the northern latitudes of the United States, the Bluebird rarely does this. The bluebirds fly in and announce to their human friends that spring is here. Through this bird, we see Alma saying that she really has an interest in the human world of which she is a part; in fact, she appears to be quite fond of the culture around her. The bluebird, like the robin, is very fond of the humans in his habitat area. Alma is unable to interact with society because of her limitations; however, I don't believe that her one-room existence diminished the productivity that she had. ***Her words*** demonstrate her inquisitiveness. She chose the bluebird to represent her warm feelings for others. The Bluebird loves to nest in hollow limbs of trees, and this is a great help to the human world because this great little tenant eats the injurious insects and worms that try to bother trees. The Bluebird society shows a great deal of domestic peace and happiness, and perhaps this was another touch point for Alma in that, probably, she desired this for human society. She enjoyed a life of security and protection, which undoubtedly brought her peace and a certain level of happiness. You and I might not define happiness in the way that Alma did; however, for her, the world must, necessarily, have been her bedroom. Without professional assistance, the world beyond her four walls was too overwhelming for her to even consider finding happiness there. In caring for its young, the Bluebird demonstrates a love for family, and Alma certainly received great care and protection from her family. We feel a wrench in our hearts when the Bluebird departs from the northern climes in the fall, knowing that the winter months will lack the gentle elegance that only the Bluebird can restore in the spring.

## Her Words

"Bluebirds sing, and I will listen. When I am with a beautiful bluebird, I feel transformed. No one knows, and no one can understand my world. I think that the birds will tell my story."

**VEERY AND HERMIT THRUSHES'**

Here are two of our most attractive and most delightful songsters. They are most easily distinguished from one another by the breast markings; as seen in illustration, the breast of the Hermit Thrush is white, heavily spotted with black. The breast of the Veery is buffy of color, and is 'smudged' with a darker shade, not spotted.

# Hermit Thrushes

The next two birds in her book offer the best glimpses of the Alma everyone met. You can spot the hermit thrush in the deep woods, but its presence is fleeting. The hermit thrush makes every effort to remain undetected. It will make an appearance, and then it will fly away as quickly as possible. The bird behaves in a modest, retiring fashion and wants no notice, if at all possible. However, many hail this bird as the sweetest of all singers. It has a pure melodious refrain that wins the Hermit Thrush the title of "American Nightingale" (Alma, 1960). The bird delivers his refrain by ascending the musical scale in rapid, repeated phrases that reach a crescendo at the end. The music of the Hermit Thrush is different from all others because it starts with a long, liquid, mellow note. His outward appearance falls short of capturing the beauty inherent in his music. Alma's outward appearance to the world was one that could easily go unnoticed. Perhaps the creature's true beauty lies only within itself, often overlooked by those who rely solely on its outward appearance. This bird is often referred to as a "swamp angel." If the hermit thrush discovers he has a listener, he becomes silent. A lot like Alma.

## Her Words

"I am sorry, little Hermit Thrush, to put you in my book. I don't think anyone will see, though. I don't think I will ever get this book finished. I know that you love and jealously guard your private existence. Don't worry, little bird of the deep woods; I will keep your secrets. Only in story will your confidence be shared, and those who read my simple words of prose will not really know if they are from my head or from your actions."

**VEERY AND HERMIT THRUSHE'S**

Here are two of our most attractive and most delightful songsters. They are most easily distinguished from one another by the breast markings; as seen in illustration, the breast of the Hermit Thrush is white, heavily spotted with black. The breast of the Veery is buffy of color, and is 'smudged' with a darker shade, not spotted.

# Veery Thrush

Alma said the Veery Thrush is known as the bird of the "silent places." He is equal in shyness to the hermit thrush. The music he makes in the song that he sings heightens the mystery that surrounds him. The song has been likened to a "spiral tremulous silver thread of music" (Alma, 1960), and in the case of the Veery Thrush, the last notes are softer than the first notes. Alma's ability to create drawings that speak for her is similar to the behavior of the Veery Thrush. There was so much to Alma, and yet the invisible barrier that kept others from entering her "silent place" (Alma, 1960) also kept her from leaving it. During the nesting period, the Veery Thrush stays in the woodlands almost all the time. Its outward appearance is not very noticeable, and once again, it is the inward beauty of the bird that truly stands out. It feeds mostly on beetles, snails, and other insects, as well as occasionally small fruits—and these are only wild fruits.

## Her Words

"I am the Veery Thrush. No one knows how much of a Veery Thrush I am. The place in my book is not important. No one will notice that this bird really is me. I am as happy as the thrush of the 'silent places.' I would like to leave my room, but I am so afraid. When I start to step through the door, it feels like I am going to faint. The floor begins to move, and the table begins to shake. Everything becomes much larger than it really is. Everything looks like it's starting to move in my direction. It just forces me back through the door."

EASTERN TOWHEE

# Eastern Towhee

Alma chose the towhee bird next, and **her words** say it well. The Eastern Towhee is also known by the common name Chewink. The sound the bird makes is very much like its name. The sound would have to be characterized by its blend of cheerfulness and inquiry. It acts very much like a ventriloquist, and it is also known for scratching the ground like a domesticated hen. Perhaps the resemblance to the hen caused Alma to make a special note of this bird. Or perhaps it was the way it acted nonchalant when something came near its nest. The cowbird often raises its young in the towhee's nest. Somehow, this bird touched her, and it meant something to her. It penetrated the invisible barrier and became one of the first to find its way into her book.

**Alma said nothing about this bird.**

BROWN TOWHEE

# Brown Towhee

The brown towhee is a shy bird that looks very much like a sparrow. It makes a metallic chipping sound. The references say the song it sings in the evening is almost like a "hymn in a temple to nature's God" (Alma, 1960). Alma believed that she had discovered this towhee on the Pacific slope in central Mexico. Although very shy, it has no real fear of men, much like Alma.

## Her Words

"I was so young once. They told me I was. Why have I grown so old? I guess no one could see me. I am like the birds. I am hidden. It's easier to be a bird. I look at my hands, and they look more and more wrinkled, with spots appearing like old, gnarled branches of the tree that some of my bird friends sit in. Sometimes I think I would like to be a tree, and then I would be around for a long, long time. I would be a home for my friends."

# BLACK-BILLED & YELLOW-BILLED CUCKOO'S

# Black-Billed and Yellow-Billed Cuckoos

The next birds in Alma's book are the Yellow-Billed Cuckoos and the Black-Billed Cuckoos. The Bible contains references to the cuckoos, and both Aristotle and Pliny wrote about them. Wordsworth wrote lines of poetry about the cuckoo. The "Cuckoo Clock" has given the Cuckoo immortality. The American Cuckoo is very different from the English Cuckoo. The American Cuckoo does not lay its eggs in other birds' nests. The American Cuckoo really doesn't sing well, and, in fact, this information might have been part of its attraction for Alma. The western part of Minnesota rarely sees the bird. So Alma must have been attracted to the bird because of the information that she found about the cuckoo. The bird wasn't a real songbird, and neither was Alma. Alma's voice was not pretty. In fact, it had a raspy sound. Because she used it so rarely, no one was really sure about the sound. The farmers in America call the cuckoo a "rain crow" because of the guttural sound that it makes and the fact that they have been credited with predicting the rain. Their behavior is ghostlike—coming and going unnoticed. The cuckoo, in fact, tries to appear absentminded. These behaviors would have won the Cuckoo a place in Alma's book, I think, because they had a kindred spirit.

## Her Words

"I move, and no one sees me. I watch my birds; they are my children. I guess I love the cuckoo. The cuckoo's transformation into an invisible figure is remarkable. Why would the clock makers use the cuckoo as the central figure of time? Maybe they thought that the clock was the perfect home for the bird. It must be something to have the whole world wait and wait just to see you come out of your house and make your announcement that another hour or half has passed. I can't go beyond my door. I guess I could not be a cuckoo. But then, the cuckoo had to be made of wood and carved by the clock maker before it was no longer invisible."

MEADOWLARK

# Meadowlark

The beautiful Meadowlark found its way into Alma's book. Perhaps Alma wished to look like the beautiful Meadowlark. Maybe that is why it got into the book. Alma's soft-brushed pastel sweaters covered her housedress. Her dress was long, and she wore thick cotton nylons. Alma lacked the beauty of her birds, but she exuded beauty from within. Her hair was piled up on her head, and she had a dowager's hump. Her uneven gait of younger years had turned into an aging shuffle. The Meadowlark greeted Alma's waiting ear every morning on the farm all summer long. She thought the song the Meadowlark sang sounded like "I-I-am-a-pretty bird." Alma loved the song. That was her song. She thought Meadowlark had no bad habits. The Meadowlark has an uncommon gait like Alma's. He neither hops nor runs; he always walks, which is not common among birds. This bird is hardy and feeds on weed seeds. It is a bird that really likes harmful insects for lunch. It sings, defines beauty, is helpful, and epitomizes the life that Alma could never have.

## Her Words

"I no longer feel so well. I wish I could go to the store with the rest. I just can't leave here. It is too much. I am not interested in going too far. I am only interested in seeing the birds that are nearby. It is easy to see why North Dakota chose this pretty prairie songbird as its emblem. I adore Meadowlark's song. I think of its song often. I hope that maybe I could be out there where the Meadowlark sits on the fence post."

BROWN) THRASHER

# Brown Thrasher

The brown thrasher is the next bird in her book. The bird derives its name from the way it vigorously twitches about its long tail when it gets nervous or angry. The bird is sometimes mistaken for a thrush. It is not even related to thrush. It is from an entirely different family, and it gets mistaken solely based on its color being similar. It may have been named Thrasher because of its actions, which look something like the thrashing of grain. It may also have gotten its name from the way it thrashes anything that comes near its young while in the nest. The Thrasher's song is truly melodic, sounding a lot like a piccolo or flute. It is one of the most beautiful singers in the entire bird world. It is known to eat vegetables, fruits, and insects. The things it eats help the environment stay in balance. It is most noticeable for its fervor and frenzy during its thrashing movements. It is not clear why this bird won a spot in Alma's book; however, my best guess would be because of the way it cares for its young.

## Her Words

"I see the way they look at me. They want me to talk to them. I don't know how. I don't know what to say. I can't look at them. I don't want them to come to my room. They told me today that the pastor was coming for me to take communion. They told me that I had to go to the kitchen. Don't they know I can't? It will be a very hard thing to do. I get nervous, like the Brown Thrasher, when I think of coming out of my room. I wish the song of the thrasher would catch their attention and make them pay attention away from me."

GOLDFINCH

# Goldfinch

It seems certain that the reason the goldfinch made it into the bird book is because of its tremendously interesting personality. The male is commonly mistaken for a canary. It seems to love people, and it loves to be right in the middle of the biggest crowd when it is feeding. It consumes a variety of seeds throughout the United States, demonstrating its true vegetarianism. When it sings, its captivating song catches all of nature's attention. It is a question whether the Goldfinch is the first on the scene when spring is in the air, or the Bluebirds and Robins. One thing is certain: the goldfinch is reckless in its pure joys that spring and summer have returned and therefore is hardly missed by anyone. Alma could not comprehend this kind of complete lack of quiet in this bird, and because of that amazement, the bird found its way into her book.

## Her Words

"Quiet little goldfinch. How can you make such a spectacle of yourself? I don't understand you. The pastor has returned. They want me to come to the kitchen. I will try, but I don't think I can. I am not afraid of the people in the kitchen. I am only afraid of the moving floor and the growing refrigerator. Everything is out of shape and lopsided. I prefer silence. Sing now, Goldfinch, go ahead, and make the world notice you."

# REDPOLL

# Redpoll

The redpoll is the next bird to appear in the book. The redpoll is the cousin of the goldfinch, and while it can sing as beautifully as the goldfinch, it does not until all of its work is done around the nest, according to Alma's notes. While the young are busy, you can only hear a faint warbling or twittering. They will feed where humans are and are not frightened. They will move closer and closer to where a human is and continue feeding as if there were nothing strange. Native to the northland, they almost always form flocks of twenty to thirty, and occasionally, two hundred to three hundred.

## Her Words

"Who knew about you, Redpoll? I think you belong in the book. I am getting weaker. I will not be able to protest going to the kitchen much longer. It will be very, very hard. They do not know the horror I face when I come out of my safe room. They will demand it soon, or I will not be able to take communion. I like Redpoll's businesslike demeanor. Why wasn't I born a bird? It will be fine with me to take communion and pray with the pastor. The birds have already shown me God."

# BLACK-CAPPED ·· CHICKADEE

# Black-Capped Chicadee

The next bird to appear in the book is the Black-Capped Chickadee. I would imagine that Alma was related to the bird because of its love for winter. It is not certain that Alma would have ever seen one outside her window. However, it is just possible that she did see one frolicking in the snow or perched on a branch, enjoying the cold of a Minnesota winter. The chickadee seems to have a gentle voice when it sings, and it is possible that Alma admired this characteristic of the bird too. Nuthatches, Kinglets, and Woodpeckers have observed the Chickadee in their company. The chickadee doesn't seem to mind hanging upside down while it is busy finding lunch.

## Her Words

"I will soon have to go out to the kitchen. I'm sure I'll do so. The pastor has come four times. I am sorry for the trouble. He would like to give communion at the kitchen table. I just can't leave my room. What will I do? I see a chickadee. The book includes the bird because it recognizes winter. I do, too. I can remember playing in the snow a very long time ago. My room is safe. I need to be safe. There are a lot of things that come back to me. The time is coming for me to go to the table. The pastor is pleasant."

TWO KINGLET'S

GOLDEN·CROWNED

RUBY·CROWNED

# Two Kinglets (Golden-Crowned and Ruby-Crowned)

Next, we find the tiny birds, the Golden-Crowned Kinglet and the Ruby-Crowned Kinglet. These two birds' coloring is fairly similar, with the exception of the Golden Crown's permanent yellow gold patch on its head. In moments of anger or excitement, the other bird only reveals its ruby marking. The kinglets are so small that only the hummingbird is smaller. You can observe these birds both in groups and individually. The two birds differ greatly in the sound of their singing. They both have very full voices for their size. They seem to have no trouble surviving a winter storm. In fact, they make themselves very busy during the process.

## Her Words

"I guess the pastor means well, so I will go to the table today. I will take communion. I pray always. I can only hope that the room will not spin, and that I will not faint. The Kinglet is another favorite. It is so small. It casts such a large shadow and makes such a beautiful sound. That is what the book says. In July, I saw God's hand in the bird's song that came to my window. I felt the heat of the day, and I heard the cool refrain of the song from my bird friend."

# YELLOW-BELLIED SAPSUCKER

# Yellow-Bellied Sapsucker

The Yellow-Bellied Sapsucker is the next bird to earn a spot in the book. This little bird gets its name because of its main activity, which is sucking sap from sap-producing trees. It will reel back its head and let it fly forward, pecking through the bark of a sap tree so fast that you can't even see it move, according to what Alma recorded in her notes. You'll surely hear the sound it makes. This little bird's tongue has a brush on the end for cleaning up sap (Alma, 1960). The hole that it places in the tree is very injurious to the tree and will cause the tree to die. They are noisy little wild birds in the spring of the year, when the sun has fermented the sap in the trees. In the fall, they are quieter and more subdued because of the change in the sap.

## Her Words

"I took communion at the kitchen table. No one knows how big my victory to get to the table was. The pastor was very nice. He doesn't realize how I remember the Bible stories. He looked at me so sadly. I think that everyone thinks I am so sad. My family just shakes their heads and looks so sadly at me. I am quite content. I feel it is my right to be. I am quiet all the time now. I will not talk, and no one will notice me. It is better that way. At least then, no one thought I might come out. I am not like the Yellow-Bellied Sapsucker. I could never be. I saw the people come, and I hid. I looked around the door, and they were staring at me. I wish they wouldn't. I don't have anything to say."

# EASTERN

## KINGBIRD

# Eastern Kingbird

The Eastern Kingbird found its way into the bird book. Alma would identify with the kingbird because it was so fearless and courageous in its pursuit of the hawks and crows. Alma must have admired the kingbird. The kingbird has a diet of almost 85 percent harmful insects. The bird provides a wonderful service to mankind in its relentless pursuit of the birds he has a good reason to hate. Kingbirds are excellent flycatchers. They perch where they can see their surroundings well. These are traits that Alma could relate to. The bird makes a very sharp and high-pitched chattering sound in flight. It would not be considered a pleasant sound to wake up to on the farm in Minnesota when Alma had her window open.

## Her Words

"I feel like the kingbird." I am not so different. The book has a section for the kingbird. People do come and visit, and I can see them. I stay out of the way. I am good at what I do. Most people do not notice what I do. I have captured my favorite birds. I really like the Kingbird because it is known for its value. I have value."

NIGHTHAWK

# Nighthawk

The Nighthawk seems to have attracted Alma's attention enough to find its way into her book. Because the sound it makes is so jarring, it cannot be considered a melody-maker. The bird is not a hawk, however. It is actually a flycatcher. Its feet are weak and its bill is weak, but it is a tremendously able catcher of flies. Some seem to refer to it as a kind of bat. This is totally false because it has no resemblance to a bat outside of the fact that it has wings and can fly. The Nighthawk's high-speed fall from high in the sky is interesting behavior. The Nighthawk abruptly descends to close proximity to the ground, producing a loud boom due to the swift airflow through its resilient wings. No one seems to really know why the Nighthawk makes this dive. It doesn't appear to have a sense of humor, so one would think that it was not just for the fun of it. However, maybe it has a sense of humor, and that would explain why Alma chose it. In her own way, she probably had quite a sense of humor.

## Her Words

"I am so interested in the Nighthawk and its ways. I think Nighthawk is very funny. This bird brings humor to my life. I guess I'd like to dive like it does just once. The onlookers that gather at my door from time to time think I am something I am not. They look at me seriously and are puzzled. They cannot decide why I do the things that I do, kind of like the Nighthawk. I am getting weary. The book is so much work. I want to finish the book. I am afraid I will not get it done."

W H I P · P O O R · W I L L

# Whip-Poor-Will

People seldom see the Whip-Poor-Will, but they often hear it. Under cover of darkness, the Whip-Poor-Will ventures very close to human habitations and makes its very familiar call. In fact, the Whip-Poor-Will's call is probably more familiar to Americans than any other birdcall. Monotony and uniformity seem to characterize the sound. Maybe that is what won this bird a place in Alma's book. Alma's life was certain of one thing, and that was uniformity and monotony. We have heard them repeat their call over a thousand times in succession. During the day, the bird is practically invisible on the ground. This is another strong similarity to Alma. The bird has the ability to make it seem like its surroundings have swallowed it. Alma seemed to have the capability to disappear in her surroundings.

## Her Words

"My fingers are sore from the needle. The quilt's pieces are nearly complete. I'd like to finish the quilt, too. Over and over, the same motion, the same action. Sometimes, I think that I cannot continue on with these projects. They are more than I could have imagined. Maybe it takes a longer time. I must work on my birds. I particularly like that Whip-Poor-Will has a place in my book. I am used to monotony, just like the bird is."

# WOODPECKER'S

IVORY·BILLED&PILATED

# Woodpeckers

This woodpecker grows very large. It is a bird that likes the quiet, deep woods. She is a great traveler. Maybe Alma chose this bird because it can do something she would never have considered. She would never have left the safety and quiet of her one-room world. However, I am sure she admired others' abilities and said so by placing this bird in the book. This bird is nearly extinct, and Alma probably felt she was helping to preserve it by placing it in the book. It is difficult to come up with a hard-and-fast explanation for the bird's almost total disappearance. The birds are very noisy during the nesting period, and they chase each other. They eat injurious insects and vegetation that humans do not depend on. Its habits all lead to a great deal of shyness and reticence. This is again a great similarity to Alma.

## Her Words

"You make your song, and I think I know what the sound is. You say, "Rat-a-tat-tat-tat," and I wonder if anyone hears you. No one hears me. I don't make a sound. I would like to join them. I just can't. My sister is here today. She is so sad when she looks at me. Why? It should be possible for me to remain here without drawing attention to myself. Does she think that I am not happy? I am happy in my safe little world. Today, I heard them talk about a sad, unhappy woman. I am glad that I am not that woman. My sister has a kind heart. She just wanted to know that I was at peace. I wish I could tell her. I just can't leave my room."

# WOODPECKER'S

HAIRY AND DOWNY

# The Hairy Woodpecker

The Hairy Woodpeckers can appear to be the big brothers of the Downy Woodpeckers. They are larger and have a similar call. Their voices are deeper and stronger; however, they are much harder to find in the wild. Both birds inhabit the same approximate area in Canada and along the northern border of the United States. The Northern Hairy is compared to other Hairy Woodpeckers. The Downy Woodpecker shares the same happy little personality that the Hairy exhibits. You can find him in the open woodlands. The Downy likes to eat tree grubs or tree parasites. The hairy enjoys insects that are harmful to the environment as well. The Downy particularly likes apples and eats a lot of them. He likes the coding moth too.

## Her Words

"I am tired. I am lonely at times. I wonder about a lot of things. I'm incorporating the Woodpeckers into my book. I like the sound they make. I can hear it through my window. The bird makes such a happy sound. My sister came again today. She is so faithful to us. I like the sound of her arrival. I like the sound of the soft conversation in the kitchen. My sister has had a different life than mine. My sister has enjoyed being around people. I wish I could let her know that I am okay."

# RED-HEADED WOODPECKER

# Red-Headed Woodpecker

The Red-Headed Woodpecker was a bird that Alma longed to see. From her notes, it is impossible to really tell whether she ever got to see it. This bird likes grasshoppers and enjoys trying to catch flies when it is flying. The red-headed woodpecker is noisier than its relatives. Its feather colors make it a very distinctive bird. People have shot this bird because of its unusually vivid colors. It does eat predatory beetles, which helps mankind; however, it also eats fruit and corn. The bird found its place in Alma's book because of its beauty and because of her desire to see one outside her window.

## Her Words

"No one understands why I prefer my room to other places. I prefer to stay away. My brother and sister are getting older all the time, and they are not feeling any better. I wish I could somehow comfort them and let them know that I am okay. I suppose the sound of a woodpecker is my favorite. I know that the sound can be irritating. It's not a sound that irritates me. It has a sound that reminds me of construction. I think the Woodpecker would be a very good builder. I guess it really isn't, though."

# Flicker

Another woodpecker, The Flicker, also made its way into her book. I believe she found it interesting, and for that reason, she included it in the book. For example, observers had given the bird many different names. The bird takes a keen interest in the world around it. I think that Alma did too. I think she was just unable to interact with others. The flicker makes an effort to form friendships with other birds. This characteristic of the bird was something that fascinated Alma. She would watch the world beyond the bedroom door and only think about the others, who seemed to be able to talk and laugh together. She was very different from Flicker in this respect.

## Her Words

"I watch, and they see, and I see. I know how I feel, and I am not strong. My quilt is almost done. It's a garden of flowers. It is my garden here inside with me. Every day, I work on my bird book. Today, I added a flicker. I think woodpeckers are interesting. I know the flicker, and I'm so different. The flicker works at making friends. I have given that idea up forever."

MOURNING DOVE

# Mourning Dove

It was probably the soft sound of the mourning dove that won it a place in Alma's book of birds. The mourning dove gives a sound that can be considered sad or loving, depending on the listener. The mourning doves construct their nests very loosely and carelessly. The wings of the mourning dove make a whistling sound while the bird is in flight. The male Mourning Dove's swift upward flight is intended to impress the female Mourning Dove. The bird has many fascinating habits, one of which is that it feeds its young through the process of regurgitation. Because it seems apparent from Alma's notes that she would have liked to have children in her life, she probably took special note of this peculiar habit of the mourning dove.

## Her Words

"The Mourning Dove feeds its young. It's not a pleasant experience. I feel that I could care for young children. I would have read the Bible stories to the young ones. The mourning dove makes a beautiful sound. I like the sound the bird makes. I think I would always want one outside my window. I cannot leave this room, but I feel safe and not captured."

CEDAR WAXWING

# Cedar Waxwing

It was probably the manners of the Cedar Waxwing that won it a place in Alma's book. I think that as she studied the bird and discovered that sometimes several will sit on a branch together and pass food along without partaking, she admired it. The bird seems to exude courtesy and kindness, if that is possible. Perhaps it was the delicate beauty of the bird that attracted Alma. Whatever it was, it is certain that she probably got to observe it from her window. On the farm, there were a number of well-kept birdhouses. As long as the farm maintained its good condition, so did the birdhouses. It wasn't until the farm itself started to show its age that the birdhouses disappeared. But by then, Alma was in bed most of the time anyway.

## Her Words

"I saw the waxwing today, and I wasn't dreaming. I think that people are not as interesting to watch and take notes on as birds are. I wonder who those people are. They came, and I felt like they were watching me. Do they hope to find a solution by watching me? There are no answers. They should watch the cedar waxwing. This bird is so kind and courteous. It reminds me of family. My family just does not really know what to do with me."

LOGGERHEAD SHRIKE

# Loggerhead Shrike

The Loggerhead Shrike is common in the southern states. It probably found its way into Alma's collection because of the fact that they are referred to as the "French Mockingbird." I am sure that Alma encountered, outside of her window, a northern shrike or two. In Alma's research papers, it was stated that the loggerhead liked to see the world from a perch on a telephone pole or a tall tree. It has a peculiar habit of impaling its prey on a thorn, and some of the research suggests that it does this because it does not have powerful feet, enabling it to hang onto its prey while it eats on it. Alma had difficulty with her feet as she grew older. Because of her dowager's hump, her gait was uneven to start with; however, her feet were probably not very strong either, making the situation worse. She didn't walk much either, and the combination of everything made it so she could only shuffle toward the end before she went to her bed.

## Her Words

"I am a little like the shrike. I make squeaky, strangling sounds. Similar to the unattractive sounds I produce, this bird, which I wish I could observe, also does not produce attractive sounds. I am safe here in my room. I don't like it when people come. I don't know many people now, and I don't think my sister and brother understand me. They are kind to me, even though they can't figure out why I stay here. My perch from which to watch the world is a good one. I am a bit like the Loggerhead Shrike; only my perch is not a telephone pole."

BLUE JAY ▼ ▼ ▼

# Blue Jay

The Blue Jay is a bird that represents everything that Alma could not do. It is known as a clown and a show-off. It is also one of the prettiest of all American birds. The Blue Jay appears to have a reputation for stealing smaller birds' nests. Even though Alma was aware of Jay's bad habits, she also found him an interesting and funny bird. Because of this bird's flamboyant nature, she probably placed it in her book. This bird can make other birds' sounds quite effectively. It really can make a beautiful sound when it decides to. Despite its reputation as a villain (Alma, 1960), people hold the Blue Jay in high regard. Alma thought a lot about this bird, and she found reference to it in a poem by James Whitcomb Riley.

## Her Words

"The Blue Jay is a bird to watch. I know some of what they say is not true. I have watched from my window, and sometimes the Blue Jay is innocent. I would watch birds all day. I love the quilt. All of the flowers are what I wanted them to be. I would love to be viewed as the 'most beautiful,' just like the Blue Jay. I am tired. My room is safe."

# WHITE-BREASTED

NUTHATCH

# White-Breasted Nuthatch

The White-Breasted Nuthatch has the same topsy-turvy habits as the Chickadee. Despite their lack of relationship, they coexist in some of the same habitats. Southeastern Minnesota, where Alma spent her life on the farm and gazed out her bedroom window, truly does not host this bird. It is hard to surmise why this bird found a place in her book. This bird prefers deciduous trees in the eastern United States. There is an outside possibility that some might have slipped into the area in Minnesota where Alma spent her life; however, it is doubtful. When it explores a tree's trunk and limbs, it can be upside down or right side up. It really doesn't matter to the nuthatch. This is possible in the nuthatch because it does not use its tail as a prop. This bird does not have the ability to dig holes in bark; however, there are those who mistake it for a woodpecker or a sapsucker. The nuthatch eats spiders and a number of different insects. It also eats nuts, seeds, and a very small amount of grain. It is a bird that does a lot of good for mankind.

## Her Words

"I saw the relatives again; they came and talked in loud voices. I enjoy the silence. From the safety of my room, I looked at them. I don't think they saw me watching them. I don't know how to get closer to people anymore. I suppose if I were like the Nuthatch, I could go right side up or upside down, and then they would notice how able I was. That is just silly, and I am very weary of thinking about what might have been. It is too scary for me to think of leaving my room to sit and talk with people. I have no idea what I would say."

# BROWN CREEPER

# Brown Creeper

I think it is quite obvious from the initial description of the Brown Creeper why it made it into Alma's collection. The Brown Creeper is known to be a rather uninteresting bird. Its feathers are neutral, and its behaviors are the same every day. It has a very faint lisping call. Alma's life became a neutral existence, and every day was the same for her. I'm sure that the Brown Creeper seemed like a kindred spirit to her. It supposedly has a very pretty call when mating, but because its breeding grounds are in Canadian forests, the call is not audible when it migrates into the United States. It eats insects and insects' eggs and spiders and spiders' eggs. It does well for its environment.

## Her Words

"I know I am quiet. I am quiet because I don't want to disturb the birds. I am quiet, like the Brown Creeper. I am neutral toward the world. I do the same thing every day. I know they want me to speak. I cannot. I suppose I could, but I will not. The woman will probably live longer than me. I wish she would be nice to both of her children. Her husband, who is also the children's father, only shows kindness to one of them. If the one child were mine, I would be joyful. I would have been a good mother. Now, children frighten me. I would have taught my child everything about birds. If you watch birds, they will tell you whether the place you live is safe."

TWO OWLS

1. HORNED OWL
2. SCREECH OWL

# Two Owls (Horned Owl and Screech Owl)

The horned owl that Alma included in her book is not one that is found in the area of Minnesota where the farm was located. This bird is identified as the "Tiger of the Air" by some ornithologists, according to Alma's notes (Alma, 1960). It's especially bloodthirsty. Like all owls, the horned owl is a nocturnal bird and hunts actively at night. It catches its prey in its very strong talons and carries it off, devouring it at a later time. It is very quiet as it sweeps through the air with its large wings. The bird is devastating to domesticated chickens and will grab them time after time. It lays eggs early in March or even February, and sometimes it incubates eggs while sitting in a pile of snow. Its most famous contribution to human society is the hooting cry it makes. There really aren't too many people that haven't heard about the "Who-Who" of the owl. The Screech Owl has a lot of the same attributes. Screech owls are known to be monogamous in their relationships, and two owls will often stay together until one dies. This bird is known for developing two very distinct colorings in its feathers: red and gray. It also does not screech when it calls. It has a soft, mournful wail.

## Her Words

"They say the owl is wise. I heard the owl at night. I know there are owls here. I think that people must think they are wise. When I watch them, I feel that way. I rarely speak at all. I love the silence. The relatives came again. They are quite noisy. I overheard them talk about a woman and a man who weren't treating their two children fairly. I do not understand this. When they are talking, I do like the sound of their voices. It reminds me of how much I like the sound of the owl's whooshing."

# LONG EARED OWL

# Long-Eared Owl

The Long-Eared Owl is, as its name suggests, a bird with long ears. It differs from other owls by the fact that it spends its daylight hours perching out in the open on trees or fence lines. It still hunts at night, just like other owls. This bird is a very silent flyer. This is a useful trait for a bird with a wingspan. It can make itself sound like a small kitten mewing or a small dog yapping. Occasionally, the bird appears in flocks. This bird is an excellent mouser. The bird is common all over the United States and does an enormous amount of good.

## Her Words

"The relatives came. I am not sure who they are. I'd love to visit with them. My room is safe. I am not going to the kitchen. I suppose they think I am a bit strange, like the long-eared owl, but it is just that I cannot come out. I would be reeling."

RING-NECKED PHEASANT

# Ring-Necked Pheasant

The ring-necked pheasant is the next bird to be included. At this point, Alma is still coloring, but she is starting to slow down. It makes me think that she is either weary or disinterested. The Ring-Necked Pheasant is native to China; however, it has been brought to the United States, where it is found in several different locations. It likes to live where there are small groves of trees and grassy areas. It likes shrubbery with bushes that grow berries. It is difficult to know whether Alma would have been able to observe the ring-necked pheasant from her window. They are beautiful birds. Their beauty might have caught her attention. They are edible birds, and it's possible that she enjoyed pheasant at their farm home in Minnesota.

## Her Words

"The sky today is very blue. It is very warm, and I was outside early this morning. At least it felt like I was outside. I left my room through the window. The sky is very clear, and I think they would like it to rain. I hear the man talk about how much they need rain. They drank coffee for a long time this afternoon. I think they like to talk, to just talk."

RUFFED GROUSE

# Ruffed Grouse

The Ruffed Grouse is in Alma's book because it was so sought-after. Hunting is a significant activity for this bird. Due to its frequent hunting, it manages to remain silent and swiftly flee. It loves to live in the dim and silent woods. I think that Alma saw her bedroom space in just this light. I think that she found it a haven out of the storms of life. Because this bird is so swift, it often escapes the hunter's gun before the hunter has even seen the bird. It is an extremely shy and suspicious bird. It watches for any signs of danger and moves swiftly. However, this wasn't always the case. During the initial years of its sightings, the bird was so obliging to humans that it would perch on a limb, making it vulnerable to a stick. This is no longer true for the bird. The nesting ruffed grouse blends in so well with its environment that it can pass over the grouse, unaware of its location. It does not leave a scent during nesting time, as noted by hunters who have had dogs miss it while it is covering its nest.

## Her Words

"My sister cares for us so well. She works very hard, and because of her labor, we are staying well. I am sorry for my brother. He is not well, either. We have our problems. I think all three of us just seem to blend in with our environment. Most people don't notice us; we are a bit like the ruffed grouse."

REDSTART WARBLER

# Redstart Warbler

The Redstart Warbler is in Alma's book by design. It has some characteristics that must have made Alma relate to it. The bird is fidgety and nervous. Some of Alma's relatives said she was very nervous and would not make eye contact with you. In fact, one relative referred to her eye movements as "eyes that darted about." She had become extremely reclusive, and perhaps the Redstart Warbler stood out to her because of its colorful feathers. The bird is constantly moving from limb to limb, searching for larvae and insects. It is by far the most fidgety and nervous member of the Warbler family. The Redstart Warbler sings a lot of different lisping sounds. The book that is the source of Alma's information on the birds says that the "bird seems altogether too busy to sing a real song."

## Her Words

"I know that the song of the birds is one I look forward to in the spring, summer, fall, and winter. I am content. No one can believe I am content. They describe living as something that entails leaving my room. I don't plan to leave my room except when I have to. I love the sound of the warblers. They aren't much for musicians, but then neither am I."

MAGNOLIA WARBLER

# Magnolia Warbler

Many of the warblers are beautiful. The Magnolia Warbler is among the prettiest of the warblers. Its black, yellow, and white coloring makes it stand out in the dense foliage of its home environment. Its movements are quick and constant, like those of other warblers. Researchers believe the bird's song lacks consensus due to its wider range of notes. In fact, many feel it doesn't have a song of its own.

## Her Words

"The beauty of this bird is my oasis. It is my bright, sparkling spring of cold water on a hot and dry day. Working on my projects is my tranquility. I'm tiring of my quilting work easily. I have a lot to do with the birds. I will be busy for a long time."

WESTERN KINGBIRD

# Western Kingbird

The Western Kingbird is the next one in Alma's book. I think that this is the Arkansas Kingbird. It certainly would be found near Alma's bedroom window in Minnesota. He stays where people can see him. He is not one bit shy. He seems to be a bird that is willing to attack other birds with great aggression. He targets owls. Hawks and crows, his natural enemies, attack their prey with great ferociousness. The bird, when he dashes from his perch, lets out a shriek, no matter if it is to attack an enemy or catch an insect. People regard the bird as beneficial to the region it lives in.

## Her Words

"The busy, busy Kingbird certainly makes its presence known. It is not quiet, either. I'm very busy, too. I continue to work diligently, but my work also shapes my potential impact. I will hope my strength endures."

CRESTED

FLYCATCHER

# Crested Flycatcher

The Crested Flycatcher has a strange habit of using a cast-off snakeskin when building its nest. No other bird is known to do this while nesting. His call has an unearthly, unmusical, discordant sound. The Crested Flycatcher does little harm, if any, and is considered very helpful to a garden or orchard. The Crested Flycatcher does not attack any cultivated ground.

## Her Words

"My days are growing shorter. I think it is because I grow tired more quickly. If someone had ever heard me sing, they might have mistaken me for the flycatcher. However, the discordant sound that I might make is kept hidden here in my Eden."

BLUE GROSBEAK

# Blue Grosbeak

The blue grosbeak is common in the southern states. He has a pretty good-looking feather coat, but he is not as handsome as his relative, the Cardinal. He is very blue, and his bill is very strong. His summer flight is taking him somewhere north. You can find the bird in short trees or bushes from Maryland to the Gulf of Mexico. His feathers' blue color does not attract attention. He might be in Alma's book because he is a very quiet bird and his singing is not particularly rhythmic. He seems suspicious of men. His song is a sweet-sounding warble, which some consider beautiful. The blue grosbeak is considered somewhat rare. Any habituated area should welcome Blue Grosbeaks as helpers, as they consume large numbers of injurious insects. After nesting, they have been known to move in flocks into grain fields, particularly rice and oats. Farmers get more help than hurt from these birds. They seem to thoroughly enjoy the tastiness of a plump grasshopper.

## Her Words

"The Blue Grosbeak is misunderstood. He sings a lot like me. I'll enter him into the book to give him a chance to tell his story. The quilt is finished."

# EVENING

# GROSBEAK

# Evening Grosbeak

The Evening Grosbeak is very easy to spot in its yellow and black feather coat. The Evening Grosbeak is considered a bird that doesn't like to be around people. The Evening Grosbeak seems to enjoy the low pine trees and ground. The Evening Grosbeak likes the buds of maple, elder, box elder, and ash. The sumac fruit is also something this bird likes. This bird's favorite food is apple seed taken from frozen apples. They don't eat insects.

## Her Words

"This is a happy little bird with a happy little song. I will see this bird in my yard, and it is the kind of bird I like. It loves sunflower seeds with a passion."

BLACKPOLL WARBLER

# Blackpoll Warbler

The Blackpoll Warbler is a beautiful songbird; however, it is hard to catch sight of. A few of the Blackpoll Warblers nest alone on the northern border of the United States. The large numbers of birds nest in Alaska, and then they travel five thousand miles back to Brazil's interior. It is one of the last warblers to travel north, as well as one of the last to travel back south to South America. The sound it makes is very distinctive.

## Her Words

"I spotted a little Blackpoll Warbler in the evergreen tree. Its black cap and white cheeks are really a sight to see. I think it stopped off for a break on its long trip. I think the song is more of a loud squeak with rhythm. It is somehow reassuring to me."

# CHESTNUT·SIDED WARBLER

# Chestnut-Sided Warbler

Chestnut-Sided Warbler probably spent summers right outside Alma's window. It is chestnut-colored and likes to eat chestnuts. It also eats insects. The bird has flourished in the U.S. and can be readily found on farms and in pastures in the area. This bird is so easy to get next to. The bird loves to sing an arresting song of speed when calling a mate or defending its territory.

## Her Words

"The chestnut bird sings outside my window. It is distinct and loud at times. Your reddish streaks and yellow forehead caught my eye. When you go home to the south, I know you remember with whom you spent time the previous winter. You love to eat the things around the farm, like insects and pinecones. I enjoy the view from my window."

CONNECTICUT WARBLER

# Connecticut Warbler

The Connecticut Warbler is a rare bird, seldom seen. It starts in the West Indies, or northern South America, and ends up in the forests of northern Michigan and Minnesota. During the breeding season, the bird has two songs. Because they forage so close to and on the ground, these rare warblers travel north and south, rarely attracting notice. It is possible that Alma spotted the bird, but not likely. The bird's intriguing anonymity likely moved her to include it in her book. However, she may have heard it singing because it is a distinctive call.

## Her Words

"What a quiet, interesting bird you are, except when you aren't. You can be loud, and your 'tweet, tweet, tweet' is amazingly sweet. I wonder if anyone sees you while you fly so quickly north and south."

# WILSON'S WARBLER

# Wilson's Warbler

The Wilson's Warbler is a quick-acting, fast-moving, fly-catching, energetic bird. He loves the cool streams in the northern United States. The black cap on this bird makes it easy to identify. This bird makes its home in the brushes that border the woodlands. The bird has an euphonious warble, usually sung far away from the places inhabited by humans. It likes berries once in a while, and it really feeds on insects.

## Her Words

"What a singer you must be, Wilson's Warbler. In the brushes, you can find. Outside my window, I watch for you. I know I will see your yellow belly and face. I will keep watching."

MYRTLE WARBLER

# Myrtle Warbler

The Yellow-Rumped Warbler derives its name from the Myrtle Warbler's beautiful feathers. It feeds on shrubbery and hedges. Compared to the other warblers, the bird stays north longer. It eats myrtle berries and prefers to live in areas with berry-growing bushes. The Myrtle Warbler has two calls: one in the autumn and one in the summer. The summer version is less musical. This bird moves less nervously than the other warblers.

## Her Words

"This bird is different from the rest of its family. I've noticed it in the books; it is a great little berry-eating bird. I'm sure I heard its sharp chirps. I'm very tired."

# BAY·BREASTED·WARBLER

# Bay-Breasted Warbler

The Bay-Breasted Warbler is a bird that lives in the Canadian Rockies. Its migration flight holds to the waters of the Missouri Basin. The bird flies a very abbreviated route to the Colombian interior. When spruce budworm problems arise, this warbler feeds well. It displays an affectation of requiescence. There is a great deal of variation in the bird's song. It has some strong similarities to some of the other warblers.

## Her Words

"This bird is a unique treasure. It is a baffling flyer, and it appeals to me that it has this baffling characteristic."

PROTHONOTARY WARBLER

# Prothonotary Warbler

The prothonotary warbler lives near running water and willows. This little bird loves a flood. It has a beautiful, sweet song. It is a very industrious bird, feeding all over the area it has chosen for its home. It stays close to its nest at all times. The bird makes its nest in the hole that a woodpecker might have made. We rarely see the bird with other warblers. It does not often go as far north as where Alma's home was, but that is not to say that it never did. She may have seen it, but it is likely that she read about it somewhere.

## Her Words

"The floods of the land attract this bird. That is natural, because it loves a swampy home. Floods are not a happy thing, but this little bird with its pretty yellow coat can make the most of anything, I think."

# YELLOW WARBLER

# Yellow Warbler

The Yellow Warbler has a distinct behavior that involves its precarious building of flooring over its eggs, among which the Cowbird has been known to lay one egg in the midst. The yellow warbler seems to be able to tell that the cowbird is laying one egg in the middle. Because of this, the warbler keeps building more flooring to keep away from the responsibility of parenting the cowbird's offspring. During this process, the yellow warbler can sometimes layer up to six levels. This little bird's yellow feathers make it one of the more beautiful songbirds. The song it sings has a lovely, cheerful sound, with short bursts or tweets at the end of its tune. It can be found among the willows that are close to the water. This is quite a well-known member of the Warbler family.

## Her Words

"Pretty you are, little Warbler, with your yellow tail spots. You're a bird of willows and water. I know my relatives like you because you eat spiders along with your berries and insects."

OVENBIRD

# Ovenbird

The ovenbird is the marching little warbler that makes its audience giggle. The ovenbird is known as the wood wagtail. The bird walks funny and bobs its tail, but strangest of all is the way it builds its nest. The bird builds the nest in an area that is almost impossible to see. When an object or person approaches a nest, the bird reacts as if its wing has broken. The bird does not sing; it makes a distinctive monotonous sound. However, the flight song is musical. The bird sings its musical song as it flies up and down, mostly at twilight. The night sound is pleasant to the ear.

## Her Words

"Great little marching funny bird in your happy pink shoes and your black stripes and orange crown, you make me smile. You fly, sing, and strut, and maybe the world will watch. Sometimes you hide your funny stuff on the floor of the forest."

# FOX SPARROW

# Fox Sparrow

The Fox Sparrow is probably one of the best-looking of the American Sparrows. It seems that among the sparrows, we find birds that dress very modestly, much like Alma. From the favorite resource book of Alma's, the Fox Sparrow soars off the page with familiarity because of its likeness to its artist. The fox sparrow feeds on the ground and scratches with both feet. It sings its song most often in the springtime. It sort of whistles its tune. The birds forage in little flocks. It consumes, among other things, ragweed seeds and millipedes. It is a great help for men.

## Her Words

"Little Fox, you are well done. I think you must be one of the best. I don't know why people don't like sparrows. If I were to sing, I would most likely whistle like you."

HOUSE SPARROW

# House Sparrow

The House Sparrow is more commonly referred to as the European House Sparrow or English sparrow. Since its introduction to the U.S. in 1850, the bird has become a ubiquitous presence across the country. The bird has flourished because it is hardy, eats a lot of different things, and has an aggressive disposition. It has almost no natural enemies. The house sparrow is an enemy of many native birds. It particularly likes to prey on those whose homes are in birdhouses, boxes, holes, etc. They have dirty habits. They frequently take dust baths. They gather in large flocks and roost in the dwellings of men. They pose significant challenges to property owners due to their lack of planning. The house sparrow grows very fast. The House Sparrow, like rats among humans, is destructive, cunning, and filthy. The house sparrow has some redeeming qualities. It eats weed seeds and insect pests, namely, cutworms and weevil larvae. It also eats fruit, vegetables, and grain in cultivated fields. People often forget how many insects these birds eat because of their noisy behavior.

## Her Words

"Oh, little House Sparrow, you seem to be hated by all. If you don't eat their grains, the farmers may learn to love you. I find you interesting from my window view. You are so busy, and there are so many of you. You are quick, and I am slow."

# WHITE-THROATED SPARROW

# White-Throated Sparrow

The White-Throated Sparrow is a very handsome representative of the Sparrows. Of all of them, it has the most beautiful song to sing. When it is on its way to its breeding ground in Canada's forests, the bird sings. The bird sings a song that many bird enthusiasts say sounds like "Oh, sweet Canada, Canada" (Alma, 1960). The White-Throated Sparrow is a ground-scraper. The bird loves ragweed and birdseed. It is considered a useful bird on the farm. Many observers have spent hours trying to figure out the song. Alma was one of these.

## Her Words

"White-Throat, the song you sing outside my window is 'Oh, perfectly, perfectly, perfectly, the world spins and I sigh.' That is what I think you say. It could be that you are singing some other ditty that I am not aware of. I love listening to you in the morning."

# WHITE-CROWNED SPARROW

# White-Crowned Sparrow

The White-Crowned Sparrow has a dome-shaped head and very distinct markings. They are very different from the White-Throated Sparrow; however, they do associate and feed together. The songs they sing are different. The White-Crowned Sparrow is not quite the proficient musician that the White Throat is. The White Crown is a sweet singer. Its songs seem to be a little shortened in comparison to the other sparrows in the field. The bird feeds mostly on weed seeds. They are a farmer's friends. They don't feed on cultivated grain crops or tame fruits and vegetables.

## Her Words

"Let the world know how much you help everyone in your world, little bird. Yes, it's true that you can sing in two languages at times. I also speak two languages. I know the words of my ancestral Norway, and I know English, but I don't sing in them like you do."

# TREE

# SPARROW

# Tree Sparrow

The tree sparrow spends most of its time on the ground. It does not even nest in trees. Its name does not represent it very well. All year round, the Tree Sparrow breeds in the North and lives in the Northern Great Plains. This bird is more than just a winter resident; it also sings a lovely winter song. Tree sparrows eat a lot of weed seeds. In a snowstorm, you can see these cheerful little singers eating seeds as they find them. Farmers really love these little buddies.

## Her Words

"I wish I had your happy attitude in winter. I get so tired of winter, but you never do. You eat any seeds you can find in winter, but in summer you eat all the insects you can find."

OLIVE=SIDED=FLYCATCHER

# Olive-Sided Flycatcher

The Olive-Sided Flycatcher has another name, Nuttall's Pewee. The Olive-Sided Flycatcher has a large living area. It is considered a common part of the forest. It is known for perching on the tops of trees. To catch an insect, the bird frequently darts almost perpendicularly to the ground from its treetop perch. Its distinctive call has sounded like many things to different people. Some say it sounds like one short high sound, followed by a long high sound, and then finished by a short low sound. Finally, it finishes its little song with three short, high-pitched sounds (Alma, 1960). It eats mostly bees, wasps, ants, and some beetles. Because of its fondness for bugs, it is a friend to mankind. The only cause of concern is if a number of these birds start feeding on the local beehive.

## Her Words

"You are in my book, happy little bug-eating companion. I know you are a complacently serene bird. You look down from your perch at me."

WOOD PEWEE

# Wood Pewee

The Eastern Wood Pewee is a pale olive color, but its call is distinctive. The Eastern Wood Pewee is a pale olive color, but its call is distinctive. Generally speaking, the only way to tell the Eastern Wood Pewee from the Western Wood Pewee is by its call. The sound it makes is like a human sigh, saying pee-a-wee, and is totally different than the fuller call of the Western Wood Pewee (Alma, 1960). The bird changes its sound in August. The bird is somewhat retiring and timid. The bird snaps up insects quickly and aggressively. Its graceful movements never miss its prey. An interesting characteristic of the Eastern Wood Pewee is that it does not let any other animals know where its nest is. This little bird eats 99 percent insects and 1 percent vegetables and berries. The one concern with this bird is that it eats too many parasitic bees and wasps. The bird does more good than harm. This bird is in some danger of reducing its numbers because of its habitat.

## Her Words

"I hear you sighing, pee-a-wee. You are so full of grace. I'm going to make you a shining star in my book."

BARN SWALLOW

# Barn Swallow

The barn swallow makes its nest on a building's side. Mud pellets, straw, grass, and an abundance of feathers line the nest. The nests they make are very dirty, and they mess up the area below the nest. They are extremely fast at catching insects on the ground. They work hard at decreasing the mosquito population. When do cats become the prey of cats on the ground when they swoop down to catch their lunch? Rodents sometimes eat their eggs. Sparrows pull apart nests to steal feathers. There seem to be fewer of these little creatures around today than at an earlier time in history. However, there are plenty of little creatures making nests on our houses and barns, in this author's opinion.

## Her Words

"Harry gets so mad at you because you are building your home under the eaves of my house. I don't mind. Your children's departure from home is entertaining to observe, despite the fact that I am aware of the mess you create. I should have been able to leave too, but I just don't."

TREE SWALLOW

# Tree Swallow

The Tree Swallow, or White-Bellied Swallow, is one of the first to arrive from the south on a spring breeze. It is one of the last to leave in the fall. The male birds come first, and the females come later, about a month to six weeks later. The females tend to stay within a mile of their nests. They are common in the Far West. They like to nest in dead trees. Some places create swallow boxes specifically for their use. English sparrows find great sport in trying to drive the pleasant swallows from their boxes. In the fall of the year, they often flock with other species of swallows, but they remain visible even after the others have left. Then, last to leave, they fly south for the winter. It is not a singer of a pretty tune. Others have likened the sound to chatter. However, it is the sound that comes loudly through your open window in early spring and throughout the summer. The tree swallow's diet is almost entirely winged insects. Tree swallows are great friends with humans.

## Her Words

"You wait and wait, little bird. You want to be the last to leave. You are a fighter. You defend your territory well. You also defend your nest like the ardent, protective mother you are. I would have loved a child to care for. No one knows my heart's color. If I had wings, I would be free to fly anywhere. I don't, and because I don't, I must stay. Your rather loud, shrill song awakens me every morning throughout the spring and summer. I like that."

TWO SWALLOWS

ROUGH-WINGED & BANK

# Two Swallows (Rough-Winged and Bank)

In this picture, Alma has captured the bank swallow and the rough-winged swallow. Like the Kingfisher, the Bank Swallow builds its nest in the ground after it has dug it out all by itself. In fact, it is not uncommon for the bank swallow to make a nest very near the kingfisher. The bank swallow feeds on insects and gets along very well with its fishing neighbor. Many of the little bank swallows will make their nests in the same bank; up to twenty or more will do so. They tend to turn the bank into a very filigree structure. They frequently locate their nests near rivers or bodies of water due to the erosion effects of the banks they prefer to nest on. They are less fond of men than their other swallow relatives. The Rough-Winged Swallow is less colorful than the Bank Swallow. It doesn't fly as fast either and does more gliding and sailing. They do nest on sand banks, but rarely more than five or six pairs in one colony. Their nests can be found along railway trestles, in old pipes, or in the deserted Kingfisher's Nest. This insect eater flies along the stream, catching all the flying insects that it can. Sometimes it will fly high in the air or over a pasture, but it rarely does so. Most of the time, it is busy catching insects along the stream.

## Her Words

"I saw you when I was very young. You were and still are one of my favorite-feathered friends. Your sounds are the busy sounds of the birds patrolling hard at work, catching insects as you fly. I can remember you well, and I am so old."

# SLATE-COLORED

# JUNCO

# Slate-Colored Junco

Some also know the Slate-Colored Junco as the Snowbird or the Dark-Eyed Junco. This cheerful little winter singer is a true bird. Junco's white-edged tail and colored hood make it stand out against the white snow. He is a friendly bird, and he is enjoyed by all who see him. People refer to him as the Black Snowbird and often spot him near the kitchen or barn doors. His familiar lisping sound can be heard all year. The Junco is one of the most common sparrows in America. In the West, there are numerous varieties of Juncos. The Junco near Alma's door in Minnesota feeds on harmful species of insects. Juncos do not harm grain crops or fruit in their habitat. They are servants to the farmers of America and should be protected.

## Her Words

"You hearty fellow inhabitant of the North, I'm not surprised that you stay here. I watch for you every day. You are so friendly, but you don't intrude. I wish people were more like you and not so concerned about how I am."

HOUSE WREN

# House Wren

The House Wren had a fascination with Alma. When you read what she wrote, you will be able to see that. People often refer to the House Wren as the fussy, little Jenny Wren. As a matriarch, the little female leads the way and decides where to build the nest. The male House Wren is the singer of the two and comes along behind, merrily singing its song. It sings very fast and is bubbly, just like it behaves. The female House Wren is a scolding little feathered influence peddler. Even though the male House Wren is quite henpecked, it still manages to sing a happy tune. Probably, after tuning out all of the scolding of its mate, the House Wren makes its nest in an old dead tree or any other such thing that resembles a cave. The house wren is entirely useful and eats a variety of insects. A house wren will make its nest in the most unlikely of places.

## Her Words

"Once I saw you in your nest. You took over that old bucket and made it your home. There were people here today, and they stared at me. I wish they wouldn't. I know that I am not that easy to look at. Staring isn't polite."

RED-EYED VIREO

# Red-Eyed Vireo

The red-eyed vireo sings constantly from high up in the canopy. It may be a drab little fellow, but its song is far from drab. Because it never stops singing, some have named it the "Preacher Bird" (Wilson Flagg) (Alma, 1960). The Red Eye is known to sit very still at times while it sings its ceaseless song. The red eye is often the bird that gets the job of parenting the cowbird. The Red Eye occasionally continues to care for cowbird babies, even after smothering and throwing its own babies out of the nest. They are nestled on a forked, suspended branch. These are birds whose wings are always longer than their tails. The red-eyed vireo is an insect that eats wild fruits.

## Her Words

"You are never quiet. On and on you go. What are you saying, bird of a thousand sounds? Who gets your sermon? I hear you, and you speak for me, too. You speak so much, I don't have to."

TWO VIREOS

PHILADELPHIA &

BLUE-HEADED

# Two Vireos (Philadelphia and Blue-Headed)

The Philadelphia and Blue-Headed Vireos are similar to their more common Red-Eyed Vireo cousins. The discovery of the Philadelphia Vireo near the town of Brotherly Love led to its naming. It is not as persistent a singer as the Red Eye. Philadelphia seems to have one note that stands out all the time and is distinctive. The bird is so plainly marked that it simply doesn't make much of an impression. Its relative, the Blue-Headed Vireo, stands out because of its striking blue head and the white ring around its eye. The northeastern states are home to this bird, known for its wild, sweet woodland song. This bird is an excellent guardian of the northeastern forests. It is a fearless hunter of caterpillars. This blue-headed vireo is a real friend to humans.

## Her Words

"Nobody notices you, Philadelphia; you are so common. Dear little Blue-Head, you are a star. Both of you are not easy to spot because some say you are drab. However, some say if they find you, Blue Head, you will allow yourself to be petted."

PURPLE GRACKLE

# Purple Grackle

The Purple Grackle is also known as the Blackbird. This bird is like a smaller version of the crow. It walks on the ground and is a very efficient nest-robber. Other birds seem to be aware of his many bad habits and have united in their view and treatment of the grackle. He seems to be the villain, even though he looks like a countryside beauty. He is not much of a singer. In fact, his sounds are the kind you might like to turn off. He squeaks more with a gravelly voice than he sings. When he eats, this bird does get into grains and vegetables. He also eats some harmful insects.

## Her Words

"Beautiful black-coated villain, if your only problem were your singing, you would have nothing to complain about. You look great, but you are a stinker, and your song makes more noise than I care for. I know that you are responsible for much of the stolen grain."

RED-WINGED BLACKBIRD

# Red-Winged Blackbird

The red-winged blackbird makes its home in swampy places. Bogs, swamps, and marshes are not usually cheerful places. The sound it makes is one of joy and happiness. It makes the listener feel like they are enjoying the spirit of eternal optimism. The males have several wives, and they breed in large colonies. There is a marked contrast between the color of the male and the female. The female is so different from the male that it could almost be mistaken for a different species. People have blamed the bird for extensive crop damage in its habitat. The bird's diet was analyzed, and it was found to contain over 70 percent vegetable matter. Animal matter made up 26 percent of the bird's diet. The bird seems to really thrive on animal matter (insects) that is harmful to grain crops.

## Her words

"Pretty Red-Winged Blackbird, your sound is so joyful. You are definitely making an effort to attract attention. Following you into the swamp would be an adventure. You sit on the cattails near the barn."

# YELLOW-HEADED
# BLACKBIRD

# Yellow-Headed Blackbird

The yellow-headed blackbird is different from the other birds in its neighborhood because of its plumage. Its plumage is so striking and unique in its color contrasts that identification is easy. When it walks on the ground, its gait is a pompous strut. The bird's arrogant superiority, evident when observed, earns it the nickname Bonaparte (Alma, 1960). It makes a squeaking, hoarse chuckle, which sounds like the bird is in pain in the process. The farmer does not view the bird with a kindly eye because it is very hard on wheat and oat crops. The bird does eat beetles, grasshoppers, and caterpillars. This is somewhat of a saving grace for the bird.

## Her Words

"I feel the pain of trying to speak with others. I want to, but I just cannot bring myself to open my mouth. I can understand this bird. When it opens its beak, it sounds like my fingernails on the blackboard."

COWBIRD

# Cowbird

The cowbird is not a good parenting bird. The cowbird is not an example of monogamy or virtue. The female cowbirds receive the males with impartial good will. Once there are offspring in the picture, the cowbird actually forces birds of other species to take on the parenting role. The cowbird is content to enjoy the summer days with a carefree lifestyle. The foster parents of the Cowbird offspring do not realize that their new parenting responsibilities will very often cause the death of their own offspring. Another interesting feature of the cowbird is its association with cattle. The cowbird inhabits areas where cattle are grazing. It uses the cattle to flush out insects that it will eat. Outside of the fact that the cowbird causes the deaths of other species of birds that become foster parents to its offspring, it can generally be considered a helpful bird. It feeds on insects and is a partner in environmental management, among many others.

## Her Words

"What an amazing bird! It is a friend to that herd of cattle. It is a bad parent on its own. He is a rascal and has no thought of his behavior being bad. They say there are many humans that are a lot like this feathered example. Parenting must not be easy. Just look at the cowbird. The tune it pipes out is really quite pleasant."

STARLING

# Starling

The starling has the appearance of a glossy blackbird with a yellow bill. It is actually so black that it almost has a purplish/bluish cast to the neck and back of the head feathers. There are many species of starlings—in fact, at least one hundred and fifty. Its short tail allows for easy recognition. During the breeding season, the bill turns a bright yellow. It is considered to be a helpful bird for farmers. It is more common in Europe than in the United States. This country greatly appreciates its insect-eating habits, beauty, and cheerful singing. Large populations of starlings can pose a threat to mature crops. The bird is a survivor; it will hold its own with life's struggles.

## Her Words

"I am interested in you, little Starling, because you can survive. You sing a beautiful tune, and it is fun. I wish I could watch you from my window. You must be fearless in battle."

BALTIMORE

ORIOLE

# Baltimore Oriole

The Baltimore Oriole is about eight inches long and very beautiful. Its upper body is sleek and black. Its underbody and parts of the wing feathers are a beautiful, rich orange or orange-yellow. Their nest-building skills are really quite extraordinary. Large elms frequently serve as the location for nests. Their nests are strong enough to be able to survive through the harshest of four winters. The female bird does most of the work while the male sits on a branch, singing and looking pretty. The bird does have a wide range of places where it lives. It is possible that Alma could have seen this bird during the summer. The bird travels as far south as Mexico, Central America, and South America in the winter.

## Her Words

"What a cheerful whistle you do for all who are willing to listen carefully. I know that I have heard you many times when my ears were listening for you. Mr. Oriole, you make a one-of-a-kind sound, and it is so beautiful. You are so beautiful too."

# SCARLET

# TANAGER

# Scarlet Tanager

Other names for the Scarlet Tanager include the Canada Tanager, Pocket Bird, Scarlet Sparrow, Black-Winged Redbird, or Firebird. The adult male is uniformly scarlet in spring and summer, with wings and tails that are uniformly black with white and a black margin. The adult female in spring and summer has yellowish olive-green wings and tails, with the underparts light yellow. The farmers love this bird because it eats the grubs, ants, and ground beetles. In the spring, Alma saw the Scarlet Tanager. When she was younger and would venture outside, she probably even saw its nest on the sapling's limb in her yard. The nest is made up of little roots, and it is brown because of this. They generally have from three to five little greenish-blue, speckled eggs in their nest. In the summer, this beautifully colored bird probably visited Alma's yard, and that is why it is in the collection. According to the information she had gathered, it appears she was able to watch this bird for a while.

## Her Words

"Little Black-Winged Redbird, some may think you are bored, but I know better. Your beautiful music and your beautiful color combine to give my spirit joy. Only once in a great while will I catch sight of you. I know you love berries and seeds, so come and eat in my yard."

SMALL

FLYCATCHERS

ACADIAN

YELLOW-BREASTED

LEAST

# Small Flycatchers (Acadian, Yellow-Breasted, and Least)

The small flycatchers were of particular interest to Alma because their jobs in nature are so well defined. These three birds catch many varieties of insects, all of which could be considered helpful for keeping the balance in the ecosystem. The Acadian makes a soft whistling sound, which sounds like it is making it with its wings. Its most common call word sounds like *peet*. Another sound that the Acadian makes is a word like *wicky-up*. The least makes a sound that is much like the name it goes by, che-bec (Alma, 1060). The yellow-breasted sound like the one-syllable word pea. Farmers and horticulturalists hold the birds in high regard due to their persistent battle against insects. The three kinds of flycatchers are very small and range in length from five to six inches. The nesting habits of each are a little different. The Yellow-Breasted make their nest in the upturned roots of trees or in fallen tree trunks on deep, shady mountains. The acadian nests in sapling forks and brushes five to twenty feet high. The fewest make their nest in the fork of saplings, sometimes on a horizontal limb. These birds are hardworking insect catchers, just as their names imply.

## Her Words

"You are the real birds of summer. Your jobs are so intense, little birds. I know you aren't very big, but the job you do is huge. I wonder how many flying bugs and creeping things end their days on the tip of your tongue."

PHOEBE

# Phoebe

Because it will build its nest on the underside of a bridge or in a sheltered area of a barn, people sometimes refer to the Phoebe as the Bridge or Barn Pewee. It is possible that Alma spotted this little bird nestling under the barn's eaves. The bird is not known for making a well-camouflaged nest. Human neighbors greatly appreciate the bird's success in eliminating noxious insects. It is not a singer, but the sound it makes is similar to its two-syllable name. Its tail-switching movement and the quick snapping of its bill when it catches an insect are characteristic of the species.

## Her Words

"Little Phoebe Bird, you are a trusted companion of the farmer and gardener. I think your nest is the one I see. You dart in and out, feeling so safe, located there in the shadows of the barn roof."

# RUBY-THROATED HUMMINGBIRD

# Ruby-Throated Hummingbird

The Ruby-Throated Hummingbird is only three and one-half inches long. Being one of the smallest birds, however, does not stop it from flying fast or hovering in space like a microhelicopter. Being only three and one-fourth inches long, the male is a metallic bronze-green with some purplish bronzy-black in color. The female is three and four-fifths inches long, metallic bronze-green, golden-green, or greenish-bronze, and faintly glossed with a purplish color. Alma chose this bird because a small hummingbird feeder hung from the eaves outside her bedroom window. There is no doubt that she found great delight in watching this bird hover while it ate from the feeder. She loved trying to see the wings moving, but because of the wings' speed, there was no way she could see them. The Ruby-Throated Hummingbird may not have been the one that Alma watched. Alma lived in an area where she only saw this particular hummingbird during the summer. The hummingbird nests approximately the size of an English walnut, perched on a branch twenty to thirty feet off the ground.

## Her Words

"You are the most fairylike of all of the birds that I watch. You remind me of what a tiny fairy in fantasy stories might actually have looked like. Oh, to fly with the freedom you do!"

# PURPLE MARTIN

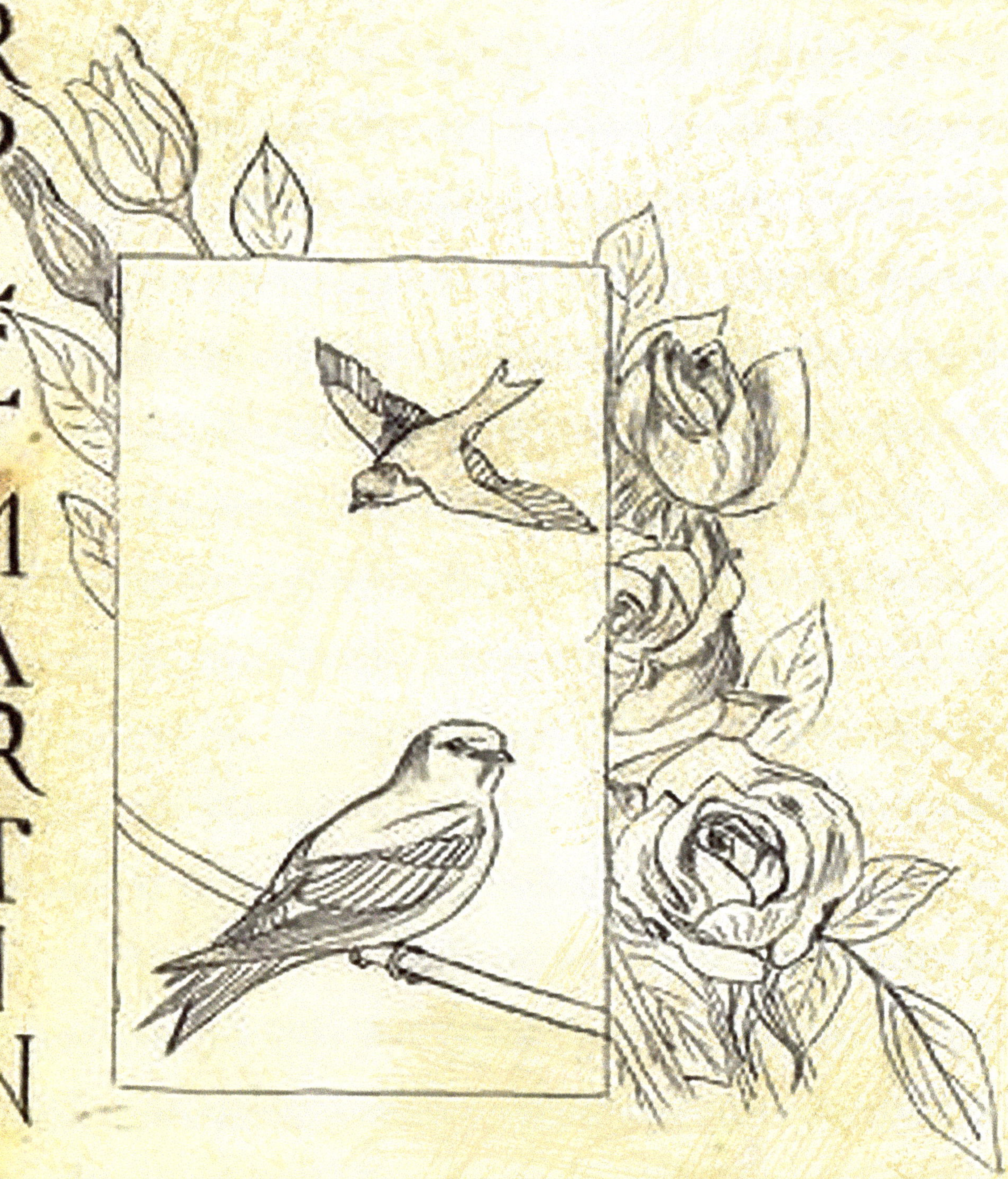

# Purple Martin

Some refer to the purple Martin as the black or house Martin. It is a rather big bird, being about eight inches long. It has a steel blue color. The male bird exhibits a particularly vibrant version of the color, while the female is much less intense in color. Lots of times, it builds its nest in boxes provided for them by landowners. The Martins' natural nesting place is in the hollow of a tree trunk. Sometimes they build their nests on buildings' eaves. Martins are considered a very beneficial bird. Their food is mostly insect-based. The Purple Martin is the most popular bird among the swallow species. The song it sings is pleasant. They are fierce protectors of their nests. Martins are a joy to have around any poultry operation because they keep the crows and hawks away. What a wonderful bird they are to have near any human inhabitation.

## Her Words

"I saw you build your nest along the eaves of the barn. I know that you really aren't supposed to build your nest there. Because you do, I can hear your happy call. You are such a good bird to help with all the work that you do."

VESPER SPARROW

# Vesper Sparrow

Other names for the Vesper Sparrow include Bay-Winged Bunting, Grass Finch, Pasture Bird, Ground Bird, or Bay-Winged Finch. This bird's length is approximately six and one-fourth inches. The bird does not exhibit a very beautiful color theme. It is grayish-brown with easy-to-see black strips. The bird's bottom side is predominantly white. The bird sings with a sound of serenity. Because it sounds so pleasant and thankful in the early evening, it is especially consistent with its name. Sometimes the bird's song has been equated with a descending series of melodic notes on a violin. This bird is very shy. It stays just out of the reach of humans but seems to be somewhat attracted to them. Humans highly regard the Vesper Sparrow for its ability to consume numerous insects that pose a threat to vegetation.

## Her Words

"You are so shy. I know how you feel. You want to see the human visitors to my home, too. I want to, but I, like you, am just a little too nervous about letting them get too close. Your song brightens my spirit. It is such a musical set of notes you pipe."

# HARRIS SPARROW

# Harris Sparrow

The Harris Sparrow has other names. People sometimes refer to it as the Hood-Crowned or Black-Hood Sparrow. The bird is seven and one-half inches long. This bird's color is also brown, with a black and white streak on its belly. The nesting grounds appear to be only in the countryside west of Hudson Bay. The bird spends half of its year in the Missouri River basin, where it inhabits dense shrubbery along the river or nearby streambeds. The Dakotas and Minnesota welcome the bird when it returns from its southward travels in early spring. Its black hood makes it easy to identify. Even though it won't be staying in this area very long, it can be heard singing its distinctive songs.

## Her Words

"I like to watch you when you arrive for your short stay here on the farm. I listen for your high-pitched whistle, but I rarely hear it. You come with a black hood that is so noticeable. After you get through nesting in the northern country, you will return with the distinctive black hood you are wearing, barely visible."

CHIPPING SPARROW

# Chipping Sparrow

The Chipping Sparrow has other names. People sometimes refer to it as Chippy, Chip-Bird, Hair-Bird, Social Sparrow, Hair Sparrow, or Little House Sparrow. The bird is about five and one-half inches long. Its color is gray, with streaks of brown and black. Its underbody is gray. The Chipping Sparrow builds its nests in trees and bushes. It likes to build its nests close to humans. The nests contain a great deal of horsehair. Its breeding grounds are located in both the United States and Canada. It is more eastern, and the southern part of the United States enjoys the winters. It seems to enjoy humans and is really curious and friendly around them. Even though using horsehair to build their nests can be dangerous, the Chipping Sparrow persists in following this instinctual behavior. This bird produces a monotonous, rapid repetition of the same note as its music. It almost sounds like a machine. People often mistake this sparrow for the field sparrow. Farmers and horticulturalists greatly love this bird. It eats almost all injurious insects and weed seeds. A flock of chipping sparrows can remove a runaway spread of crab grass with great efficiency.

## Her Words

"I am sure that I saw you today. I remember hearing your song. You sound a little like me when I sing. You pick a note, and then you sing the same note over and over. You're a bit like a rapid-fire machine. You are a favorite among our farmer friends. You greatly assist the local landowners. I am so proud of you. I hope I'll have time to color you in. I am weary."

# SONG SPARROW

# Song Sparrow

The Song Sparrow is also affectionately called the Silver Tongue, Everybody's Darling, Ground Sparrow, Hedge Sparrow, Bush Sparrow, Ground-Bird, Marsh Sparrow, Red Grass-Bird, and Swamp Finch. The bird is generally about six and one-half inches long, with its upper body brown-and-black streaked, while its underbelly is white with black streaks. It builds its nests on the ground in fields or near wooded areas. Grease, leaves, and stems make up its nest structure. They then line the nest with fine grass and hair. This is one of the better-known sparrows. It is not as sure of men, so it prefers to live along roadsides and out in the fields. Most humans who pay any attention at all to the songs of the sparrows can recognize the music of the song. The refrain the bird sings is both simple and varied each time the bird sings it. The song's beauty and simplicity make it the hallmark of this truly lovely bird. Its markings are distinctive, with strong markings on its breast and its slightly forked tail, which show when it flies. For most of its diet, the bird eats noxious weeds, and the rest consists of insects. It is a well-thought-of bird by the humans who occupy the same space. Many of these birds are scattered throughout the map. In each location, they are a little different in color.

## Her Words

"I love the sound you make, beautiful Song Sparrow. Each time you call, it has a little different sound than the time before. I think you're praying as you throw your head back to release the beautiful notes from your throat. I am pleased that you came to the ground outside my window. Your intentions all seem to be good. I will watch for you in the winter because you very often stay and cheer me through the dreary gray days."

TWO HAWKS

(1)

(2)

(1) RED-TAILED

# Red-Tailed Hawk

The Red-Tailed Hawk is sometimes referred to as the Chicken Hawk or the Buzzard Hawk. The bird is about twenty-two inches long and is dark brown with a white underbelly. It builds its nest forty to eighty feet above the ground in the fork of a large, sturdy tree. Large sticks form its construction, and smaller, more supple twigs line it. It makes a sound that captures our attention as it flies in circles above the ground, catching its savory mouse dinner. This hawk very seldom raids the chicken yard if it has plenty of mice, squirrels, and other little four-footed beasts. The Great Plains undoubtedly host this hawk, and Alma's farm was undoubtedly its home. Sixty-six percent of the Red-Tailed Hawk's diet comes from injurious small mammals, and very little comes from poultry.

## Her Words

"You are such a helper here on the farm. I can sometimes see you perching on the pole beside the barn. Sometimes, I look at you twice, thinking you might be an eagle. I know that you are hoping that some little four-footed beast will find its way into your clutches. Your grace when you fly, great bird, is like watching poetry."

TWO HAWKS

(1)

(2)

(1)-BROAD-WINGED

# Broad-Winged Hawk

The Broad-Winged Hawk found its way into Alma's book because she would have occasion to see this hawk near her window looking out on the farm. It is also referred to as the Broad-Winged Buzzard. The Broad-Winged Hawk likes to live in the deep woods. The male is about fourteen inches long, and the female is about eighteen inches long. Its wingspan is thirty-three to thirty-eight inches wide. Its underbelly is white with a pattern of brown markings on top. The bird's top and back are blackish brown. The bird tips its white tail feathers. The bird has the ability to sit motionless for hours. This behavior reminds me of Alma. She could lay or sit motionless for hours, too. The bird appears to be asleep while it is sitting motionless. It is not. It is fully awake and watching for the slightest movement. If the bird sees some movement, it flies off like a dart and attacks its victim with no apparent remorse. Alma would sit and observe for a long time. She wasn't missing anything at those times. By the flickering of her eyelids, one could tell she was just silently observing. She would then move on to write or draw, and there was a directness that told you she had been assimilating all she had seen and had somehow applied it, according to her sister. The Broad-Winged Hawk would be considered a helpful bird. The bird primarily enjoys eating mice, frogs, and other small animals. The bird does eat toads and snakes. This part of its diet is not helpful, but it does not overshadow all the good the bird does.

## Her Words

"I have observed your cunning silence. Some might think you are asleep, but you are watching and waiting. I am like you. They believe that I am asleep or not watching. I am. I see."

TWO HAWK'S

(1). GOSHAWK

# Two Hawks (Goshawk)

The goshawk goes by other names, such as Blue Hen Hawk, Blue Darter, Partridge Hawk, and Chicken Hawk. It is a large bird, with the female measuring twenty-four inches and the male measuring twenty-two inches. This bird has a black back and head, as well as a white underbelly. This hawk typically nests in deep woods. It is usually very high up in a conifer tree. This bird is a raptor, and because of its strong drive for food, it is lacking in caution. Because of the young goshawk's coloring, its naughty deeds are often attributed to the red-tailed hawk. This bird exudes beauty with its symmetry and body form. This bird is very daring. It will go after its prey, even if some other hunter has already captured it. This flamboyant behavior will sometimes bring about the death of the goshawk.

## Her Words

"Beauty describes you. You are the soaring machine in the blue sky. You are always interested in food. You are never satisfied. You are loud and arrogant in your call. I have such a desire to watch you, and it just does not happen very often. At this moment, are you watching the chicken house? I know that you will succeed in your quest."

TWO HAWK'S

(1) ROUGH-LEGGED

# Rough-Legged Hawk

This hawk is quite large, ranging from twenty to twenty-two inches long. Its earthy tones of black, white, and gray complemented the type of birds Alma was most fond of. The parts of the farm that appealed to this bird the most were the open meadows and brushy places. The hawk could spot lemmings and mice with ease.

This bird found it most occupying to stay in an area of a meadow for quite some time, controlling the rodent population of smaller-sized animals with ease. Farmers in the area loved to have the Rough-Legged Hawk build a nest in a tall tree or on a ledge. This ensured the farmer would have help controlling the little destructive creatures with the fast-flying wings of the rough-legged hawk.

***This hawk is highly valued by those who depend on the farm for their livelihood. The bird's unwavering, enduring willingness to work through the night made it extremely valuable.***

## Her Words

"You are the biggest and most regal of the hawks I can see. I love watching you swoop down and get mouse after mouse with real ease. With only two or three eggs in your nest, you have to be strong and willing to keep doing your job against all odds."

TWO HAWK'S

COOPER'S

MARSH·HAWK

# Cooper's Hawk

The Cooper's Hawk is also called a Pigeon Hawk, Chicken Hawk, Quail Hawk, Big Blue Darter, Swift Hawk, or Striker.

The male is eighteen inches, and the female is twenty inches. The wingspan ranges from thirty to thirty-six inches. Their color is blue-toned slate. They typically build their nests in tall trees, which often grow quite large, and continue to use them for many years in succession. It has about three to six blue- or green-colored eggs. Reddish-brown spots often adorn the eggs. Cooper's Hawk is a fierce and destructive predator. It will swoop into a farmyard and grab a chicken right in front of humans. There is never time to catch the thief because it comes and goes so quickly. It is known for being so much more destructive than other hawks simply because there are so many of them. It loves to eat chickens, grouses, cottontails, and domestic doves.

## Her Words

"You are a thief of the helpless, but I really like your swiftness and power, oh bird of prey. When you make your call, you are loud and fearlessly assertive. You choose your next meal, and off you go with neither man nor beast able to stop you."

TWO HAWK'S

COOPER'S

MARSH HAWK

# Marsh Hawk

The Marsh Hawk is generally around nineteen inches in length, with a wingspan of from forty-five to fifty-two inches. Males are lighter ash brown on the upper part of their body, with the underpart white. The females are dark brown on the upper part and brownish-white below. The young birds are similar in color to the adult female bird, only they are darker everywhere. They build their nests of fine, dried marsh grass in a thick growth of weeds. Sometimes they lay as many as nine eggs, but usually four to six eggs of dull white with a light dust of a greenish or bluish color. Occasionally, a faint pale brown tint blotches the eggs. This hawk searches the fields just as if it were following a military precision grid. It sees every bit of the field where it is searching for its next meal. It comes to an almost complete halt, and then it dive-bombs its target. Quite often, the speed of its dive causes it to miss its dinner. However, once it establishes a connection, the Marsh Hawk promptly consumes the squirrel, mouse, lizard, frog, snake, or rabbit. When a male Marsh Hawk attempts to catch the female's attention, it flies in great semicircles that become tighter and tighter as the hawk flies. Then it suddenly comes to a stop and falls head over tail, and at last, before hitting the ground, it flies out and up. Both the male and female help with the care of the young by defending them from enemies. Once it has completed its responsibility of teaching its young to fly and hunt, this is a flocking bird. During the time the young are in the nest, the adult hawks can destroy one thousand field mice.

## Her Words

"You are so good to your little ones, March Hawk. You get rid of so many mice around our farm. I've only seen you once down by the old pond. I wish I could watch you fly. You have a short staccato call, but it is loud."

SPARROW HAWK

# Sparrow Hawk

This hawk is not very large in comparison to other hawks in the family. Alma found it interesting that the smallest of the Hawk family was also the most sociable. I think that is the reason the bird found its way into her bird book. No doubt, it nestled in a nearby tree on the farm. She probably watched it play its hovering game with mice and grasshoppers on the farm and was delighted when this most social of hawks had success clutching a mouse or snatching a grasshopper. Alma asserted that people consider these hawks to be the most helpful. They rarely go after chickens or other small birds. They are much more prone to grabbing the kinds of pests that bother the local human inhabitants of the same environment. It seems to be a real fan of spiders, caterpillars, and beetles. These pests also bother farmers and other human cohabitants. During the late fall and early winter, these helpful, talented pals seem to love the meadow and house mice that they can capture, winning big accolades from the humans in their world.

The open holes in trees forming the most envious nesting situation for the Sparrow Hawk meant that the nest of a Sparrow Hawk in the yard on the farm was not only probable but also seemed to be a certainty, according to Alma's brief comments. The hawk has nondescript eggs in the nest but lays enough to ensure that its offspring will survive. This hawk does not have any fancy markings or outstanding colors to distinguish it as a beautiful bird, but it does have the personality and hunting instincts that endear it to its human cohabitants.

## Her Words

"You are the one I watch a lot. I have seen you hanging in the wind as if your wings were merely decorations. I know you are beating your wings so fast that it is unimaginable to most of us. I love what you do for us. I love that you found the mice on the farm—a meal you enjoy. Any grasshoppers you catch are less likely to bother the garden, and we owe you a lot."

KILLDEER PLOVER

# Killdeer Plover

Other names for the Killdeer Plover include Noisy Plover, Chattering Plover, and Killdeer. The bird measures about ten inches in length, with an olive-brown top and a pure white underside. This bird has four black bands. There are two on the head and two on the breast. It just lays its eggs right on the bare ground, oftentimes in a field and near water. They are just dull beige with a little brown speckling.

It is a noisy bird that runs and flies everywhere, calling its own name. It feeds on bugs, worms, and grubs. It acts nervous while on the ground, and it is constantly screeching its own name. Despite its usefulness, we should never hunt it, as its flesh is not edible. It is a fierce protector of its young. When it flies, it is a very beautiful bird to watch. It has huge economic value to farmers because of its love of noxious insects such as mosquitoes and grasshoppers, just to mention two of the many it enjoys.

## Her Words

"Everyone claims you are noisy and obnoxious, but I like your sounds. I understand that when you are constantly calling your name, things are fine. Harry says, You seem to be running in circles, and then you just fly in circles."

KING RAIL

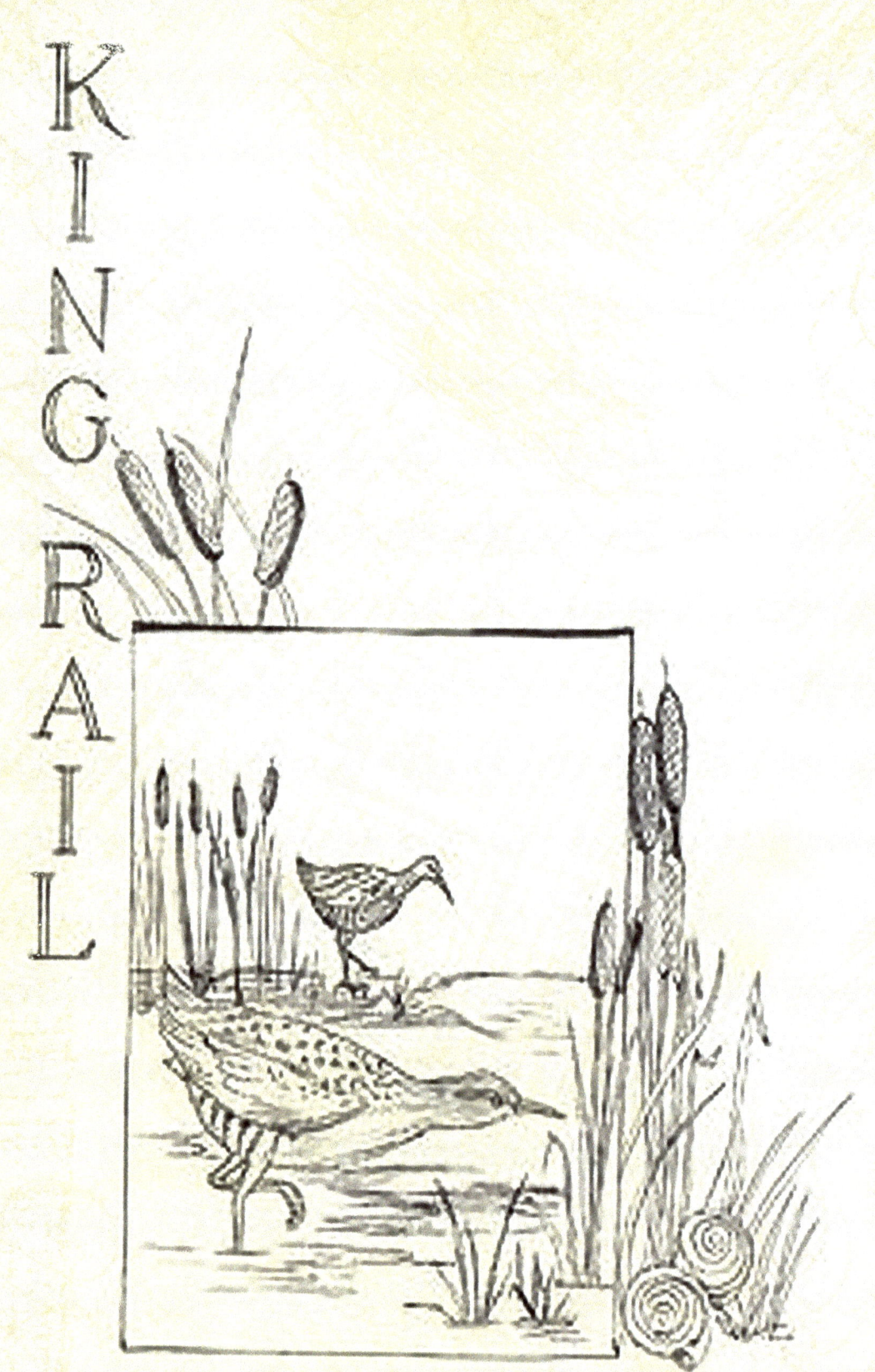

# King Rail

From the one source that I believe Alma used, there was not a lot of research completed about this bird. They seemed to know the bird had secretive habits, which kept it out of most humans' viewing range. At the time Alma was doing her research, they seemed to know that the birds preferred fresh marshes to salt marshes. They'd tracked the bird's size and description. The bird measures nineteen inches in length, and its color range includes olive, both light and darker, chestnut, blackish brown, and white, with its legs being a pale greenish color. On the ground, the bird nestles in the marsh grass. They did identify some interesting characteristics of the bird. Many of the birds nested in close proximity, and they observed some females laying their eggs at precisely the same time each day, a phenomenon they found to be very interesting. Studies conducted and reported by Alma likely indicate that the birds consume seeds and grains. It was a bird that would have been in the area where Alma might have seen it at some point in her life, but we will never know the answer to this question.

Alma had nothing to say about the bird.

AMERICAN BITTERN

# American Bittern

It is twenty-four to thirty-four inches long, with brownish white and some black on top and underneath a yellowish color. The bird seems to enjoy life in the slimy bog. It nests in marshy, boggy places. It does venture into large meadows in search of grasshoppers. In the marshy reeds, the bird's color blends into its surroundings. It can play possum very well. The bird produces a unique hiccough sound by violently jerking its head and neck. This is probably its most distinctive characteristic. The bird seems to swallow air, and the sound resembles a burp. Snakes or muskrats often steal the young.

## Her Words

"You smart little bog bird. Your looks are deceiving. I know there are many who would like to be like you. Is that you burping, or is it your call?"

GREAT BLUE HERON

# Great Blue Heron

People also refer to the Great Blue Heron as the Blue Crane, Crane, or Common Blue Crane. It is approximately forty-six inches in length. The color on the top of the bird is grayish-dark blue, and on the bottom of the bird it is black.

Usually, the bird builds its nest in tall trees. You will often see these nests near running water. It'll lay three to six blue or greenish-blue eggs. The bird is destructive to the game fish's spawn and young. Its other prey include frogs, crawfish, small snakes, and salamanders, among other small creatures. The bird is believed to be the largest of the American herons. People view it as a stately, dignified, and beautiful bird. These birds are very alert and farsighted, so getting up close to them is very difficult. The bird is an amazing hunter, as it can spot grasshoppers and meadow mice with ease. This great fisherman stands in the water like a statue until his prey is close enough to strike, at which point he strikes and rarely misses. These birds form colonies during the breeding period. They build very large nests and raise their young in this group form of living.

The Herons regurgitate food for their children. A pair of Herons with four or more young can eat twelve to fifteen gophers per day.

## Her Words

"Great Blue Heron, you are a crafty eagle-eyed hunter. You sit like you are sleeping, and then you strike so fast that I cannot see you move. No one notices you when you sit like a statue, but you see everything. If you could speak, I would talk to you about the idea of throwing food into your babies' mouths. I just don't understand. Oh yes, and your call sounds like a small dog's bark."

HERRING GULL

# Herring Gull

Other names for the Herring Gull include the Common Gull, Harbor Gull, Seagull, Lake Gull, and Winter Gull. The bird is about twenty-four inches long. Its color is white and grayish-blue in adults. Their coloring is a little duller in winter. It is doubtful what Alma would have thought of a glamorous environment. She may have found them interesting, which is why she included them. She likely found the possibility of playing with them fascinating. The old birds will kill the young birds by pecking their heads. The young birds are not able to distinguish the parent bird from the other adults, so they sometimes die trying to get food from the wrong adult.

## Her Words

"Herring Gull, your babies die because they do not discriminate. You must teach them the dangers of approaching an unknown adult. You know, 'do not talk to strangers,' Herring Gull."

# COMMON TERN

# Common Tern

The Common Tern is also called Sea Swallow, Wilson's Tern, Summer Gull, Mackerel Gull, Lake Erie Bass-Gull, and Redshank.

The bird is fifteen inches long and is a great fisherman. It has a white and pearl-blue color scheme. These birds do not need much of an indentation in the sand to make a nest. They happily line their nests with grass and dry seaweed. Common terns live in colonies. Sometimes it changes its nests according to the environment in which the tern lives. They fish by plunging their heads underwater to catch their prey. Their prey includes small fry, shrimp, and other small crustaceans, as well as grasshoppers and other insects.

## Her Words

"Little Common Tern, you float when it's hot, just like a real bather. You make all kinds of wild noises as you do your fishing. You make short calls and long calls. You are interesting."

MALLARD DUCK

# Mallard Duck

The mallard duck also goes by the name "common wild duck." This duck is not an extremely large duck, but it really is a pretty duck. Imagine a bird with a glossy green head and upper neck, adorned with shades of purple and deep Prussian blue around the neck, and a white ring, and you'll be astonished by the bird's vibrant touch. Its back is grayish-brown, with more brown in the center and on its shoulders. The lower back, rump, and tail are glossy black, with the tail mostly white and the center feathers curved. It seems to form two black and two white bars of color with a silver-gray underbody; its bill is olive, and its feet are orange-red. Its iris is brown. It builds its nest on the ground in grasses and weeds, lining it with fine reeds, grass, or leaves. It will have six to eight eggs in a beige-green color. The Mallard is by far the most well-known duck in the Northern Hemisphere. For thousands of years, it has provided people with both meat and eggs. Many countries, particularly in China, domesticate the mallard, relying on it for a significant portion of their food needs. It is a great propagator of its own kind, so there has rarely been a shortage of ducks.

## Her Words

"The Mallard reminds me of many of the men I have observed from my home. He is wary, wise, handsome, and strong. I would welcome a man of the Mallard nature into my life, but it is not to be. Because it is such a hardy bird, it has spent many a winter right outside my window in the open water of the stream. It would be a heartwarming lift to you if you took time to study my friend the Mallard."

TWO DUCK'S

BLUE-WINGED TEAL

Bufflehead

# Two Ducks
# (Blue-Winged Teal and Bufflehead)

The Blue-Winged Teal only makes its appearance in the summer this far north, and it is rarely seen out the window of Alma's room. However, Alma found a passion for knowing something about the bird. She wrote, "Teals might be called the little guys of the duck family." The teal can scramble into the air, much like a jet taking off from an aircraft carrier. It is the most graceful bird that more bird-watchers can ever recall seeing. The eye follows the bird's wing with its white, black-edged crescent patch near its eye set in a brownish patch of feathers; the eye follows the wing of the bird; and there is another patch of slate-gray blue. It builds its nest on the ground, in grass, or among the willows. It lines its nests with down. It often has up to eleven eggs in a buff color. It is a prolific little duck. The Blue-Winged Teal is not as hardy as its relative, the Green-Winged Teal, but it survives well in the northern climes. The blue-winged teal seems to be quite common among those of us living on the prairie. This duck actually likes our marshy little ponds behind the main farm.

## Her Words

"I have given my life to watching and researching birds. I believe the ducks have brought me as many laughs as any of the other humorous birds I've watched. I know one thing: the blue-winged teal mom never flies directly to her nest. She always flies a diversionary route before she comes in for a landing. She has to have mostly brains in that tiny little cavern of hers, called a head."

# Green-Winged Teal

The Green-Winged Teal has roughly the same color mix, but instead of blue, there is the prettiest green. There are not very many of these lovely birds left in the eastern part of the United States. These awesome animals prefer the less-populated prairies, and "I am fortunate that the window of my room opens onto a world of birds living freely." The Green-Winged Teal stays longer in the northern states because of its harder constitution. It breeds in open-water areas and will stay there for as long as the water does not freeze over. This bird actually likes the more alkaline ponds and seems to prefer to breed on the northwestern side of the United States. The teals might be considered smaller by comparison to other ducks, but they are hardy animals with great survival strength.

## Her Words

"I am weak and weary, and my days are growing short. I have watched the ducks in spring, summer, and fall, and I have found them to entertain me when nothing else could. Within the large circle of my feathered friends, I find joy. Through them, I have not felt it necessary to have too much to do with people. I have been frightened of life, so I chose not to live it except through the lives of the birds I have gazed upon. Writing this has helped me, and now I will file it away. I've never had to argue with anyone about my political beliefs. I have never had to justify my space in life. I may have lived a simple life by some standards, but don't let that fool you. The wickedness of the constantly coughing world has not troubled me. I am not impressed by Hollywood, and I don't believe their words will last that long. The man who watched the birds observed the real images of life. I am impressed by him."

# Bufflehead

This duck was another of the special creatures that made it into Alma's book of birds. This duck has a lot of reasons for making the cut. It has a large, fluffy head, which is reminiscent of the buffalo that roamed the prairie during much of the history of the area around the farm. The duck is an excellent diver and escapes the hunter's gun with ease. This duck probably fed on crawfish, leeches, snails, and grasses in fresh water. It also eats grasshoppers and locusts, as well as many other insects, some fish eggs, and fish food.

Alma discovered that this duck shared some of the characteristics of the birds she wanted to highlight in The Bird Book. This duck has so many unique characteristics. One of them is escape from danger. When danger comes near, it would rather make a run for it in the water than try to fly away. This duck is known for being somewhat plump. The duck is careful about reproducing by laying in excess of nine eggs and nesting them near the water in a hole in an old tree or something similar. The males are black above and white below, whereas the females have a dull grayish tone and are very nondescript. However, the Bufflehead is a serious contender for the position of "favorite" in Alma's world, and her few words demonstrate this.

## Her Words

"From the moment I started watching you, I could not believe how well you fit into my book of special birds. I like so many things about you. I used to watch you and found you to be a lot like me. You do not fit the 'duck mold.'"

BELTED KINGFISHER

# Belted Kingfisher

I can only imagine what might have caused Alma to include the Belted Kingfisher in her book of birds. She left no words to provide any kind of clue. In studying the Belted Kingfisher, I found that it is a gregarious bird, and this is something Alma most certainly was not. It has extremely good eyesight, and this might be a similarity to Alma. The Belted Kingfisher seems to be quite territorial and strong-willed. These two characteristics might also be two that Alma evidenced quite openly in her own personality.

The rather dull metallic bronze-green and white collar around the neck of the bird may have intrigued Alma. She would probably have seen it as rather "plain Jane" in the bird world. On the surface, Alma was a bit of a plain Jane, but she had many sharp and deep-seeded abilities that no one would notice at first glance. This seems to be a lot like this particular bird. The bird's look would not have drawn attention, but rather its sharp fishing ability. Not only can the bird see the fish under the water from a great distance, but it can also catch or spear the fish with its long-pointed beak. I am quite sure that this was most impressive to Alma. The only way anyone would note such deep rivers in Alma would be if they spent a good amount of time watching her work from a vantage point that would not bother Alma. This, too, would be true of the Belted Kingfisher. It is a bird worth observing in action to truly appreciate its exceptional qualities. There has to be a reason why this bird was the last one in her book. However, like so much about Alma, we will never know, because with this bird there were no "words from Alma." We cannot talk to her about why she included this bird, and the bird is far more than it seems at first glance. Alma's life was characterized by mystery, and the inclusion of the final bird in her book reflects this mystery.

# Epilogue

So ends the journey through Alma's bird book. She finished her quilt of the states' flowers. She compels us to wonder. At first, I thought, Who would read such a book? It is not all my writing, nor is it all Alma's writing. She and I are as different as night and day, and yet we share some commonalities. I am intrigued by the plethora of upbeat, positive thoughts she has entwined in her somewhat lonely existence. We often use appearances, which are not accurate, to judge the day and its people. My little part in unearthing this journey through the birds and quilt pieces is really nothing by comparison to her labor. I had a quilter finish her work with backing and stitching. She worked on the book from 1960 to 1980. I held the book for many years, and in 2010, I decided it is time to share this story. Perhaps her simple thoughts and my simple additions will encourage someone who is not so much like everyone else. Putting this book together was very much like a jigsaw puzzle. Perhaps her pictures will evoke a gentle, wistful emotion in a quiet, thoughtful viewer. Perhaps, just maybe, the bird pictures will inspire readers to pay more attention to our feathered friends. Our world sometimes seems out of control. However, we can control our own outlooks and approaches to the world around us. She may have had a far better understanding of who God is than those who seem to have all the answers. She took note of Creation and zeroed in on the pleasant peaceful bird population instead of fretting and worrying about the world of chaos that erupts from time to time. She knew the Bible and knew that the scripture talked about the birds.

Matthew 6:25-27, 34 "Look at the birds of the air; they do not sow or reap or store away in barns, and yet your heavenly Father feeds them. Are you not much more valuable than they? Who of you by worrying can add a single hour to his life? Therefore, do not worry about tomorrow, for tomorrow will worry about itself." (NIV)

Psalm 104:12"The birds of the sky nest by the waters; they sing among the branches," (ESV)

Job 39: 26-30 "Is it by your understanding that the hawk soars and spreads his wings toward the south? Is it at your command that the eagle mounts up and makes his nest on high? On the rock he dwells and makes his home, on the rocky crag and stronghold. From there he spies out the prey; his eyes behold it from far away. His young ones suck up blood, and where the slain are, there is he."

And finally:

Isaiah 40:31 "But they that wait upon the Lord shall renew their strength; they shall mount up with wings as eagles; they shall run, and not be weary; and they shall walk, and not faint."

The ending is what you make it to be. Her story is not complete, but I think that is okay because all of us deserve a modicum of privacy, and she ensured that hers would always be. Be blessed by her birds.

# *Credit*

Of course, Alma gets the first line of credit. This book is a shared work by Alma and me. It was important for me to not let this one woman's life go unnoticed. So I gathered together the few words she had written. I believe she could have derived most of her thoughts and words about the birds, either directly or partially, from the book. Birds of America

Garden City, New York
Copyright, 1917, by
The University Society, Inc.
Copyright, 1936, by
Doubleday & Company, Inc.

I believe this because I have found some similarities, so I want to give this book credit for the thinking that may have been the foundation for Alma's thoughts about the birds. It could have been the guide she used, but she also appears to have made reference to Audubon in her writing.

## Author's Note

It's possible that she also used other sources. However, I would have no way of knowing how to give further credit to any other author. I'm confident she possessed numerous beloved bird-related books, but they weren't among the items she sent me. I believe what is important here is the fact that she painstakingly drew these birds and then researched them a bit, along with equating some of their characteristics to her own. It is evident that no one poked, prodded, or overanalyzed her. They allowed her to lead a life that, in today's fast-paced world, might seem painstakingly dull. In our world, so many people live very shallow lives, with great excess, and with little regard for others in the process of their pleasure-seeking lives. While this one woman seemed to require very little by worldly standards, she was able to make a contribution of great beauty and estimable words conveying good thoughts. I have enhanced and added to her research, so Alma and I share the work. It was a pleasure to bring her birds, her quilt, and her few words together in a type of story without an ending. I guess it is up to you, the reader, to finish or imagine the rest of her story. I think she might have been a good friend to get to know. She appears to have been an observer, musing about the world she saw from her bedroom door and windows. There are politicians and celebrities on all sides with their many mansions, gilded jets, and pompous ways telling us to live the "simple life" and that we will be better for it. I would like for them to learn a lesson from Alma. In truth, these same arrogant individuals would not recognize a "simpler life" if it came up and planted itself squarely in front of them. They would simply show disdain and disregard for such individuals. This one woman, in all of her "plainness," recognized a great deal more than the many who live life largely with no regard for anything around them, only for what satisfies and pleasures them. That is why I felt it was important that Alma's life be remembered. We can learn from **her words** because she lived with so little of this world's material allurement. There is a lesson here for all of us.

"Alma's Quilt."

# Author Biography

Patsy Levang was born and reared in Western North Dakota. She attended North Dakota State University where she graduated with a degree in psychology. She attended graduate school at the University of Kansas. After a thirty-two-year career in the education, She and her husband, Gary, are retired and living on their farm near Watford City, North Dakota. Patsy and Gary have three married children, and seven grandchildren. Patsy is currently involved in fighting to keep Title-9 in place for women's sports, and all other places and spaces for women only. Her volunteer experience includes sorority, healthcare, over forty years of church service, and having started and run a school for 30 plus years, she is now dedicating much of her time to writing.